A REAL PERSON

A REAL PERSON

Life on the Outside

Gunilla Gerland

translated by Joan Tate

SOUVENIR PRESS

. . . then I understood that the improbable is
what actually happens
and that there are so very many prejudices
about the truth

Torgny Lindgren

Contents

1   The Beginning   9
2   Continuation   201
3   Now   241

1

The Beginning

One

An early memory:

I am sitting on the floor in the nursery. In front of me is a toy, a kind of board with oblong bits of wood in various colours. There are holes in the board and the wooden pieces have to be banged in with a mallet that goes with it. I bang the blocks in and am aware of nothing but what I am doing. I am sitting facing the wall and there is nothing beyond what I am doing. No world. Only me and what I'm doing. I wish there were more blocks so that I could go on banging down new ones instead of having to pick up the old ones. Before the blocks drop out, they slide down a curved track. I love that curve. I love seeing the blocks coming down that curve. Again and again. As long as I like.

My love for curved things began early, long before it became so vital to hold them. I liked bends—they were so soft and, well, curved. I felt a need for them and they gave me some kind of satisfaction. A curved thing had something calming about it, a wholly obvious feeling. A curved thing was calming in the same way as green was green—so obvious it was impossible to explain.

To the world around me, my behaviour was utterly incomprehensible. I kept touching things all the time—poking my fingers into or under bottles, sofa arms and door-handles, rubbing my palm against turned banisters. I simply had to touch all these things that had the curve I needed. But no one around me had any idea it was the curve in particular that was the common denominator in everything I had to touch. I did nothing but a whole lot of strange and occasionally irritating things. I didn't know

11

that what I was doing was odd and annoying to others. All I knew was that what I did, I did out of necessity, vital necessity. And that in the eyes of the world around me, this aroused no respect.

I had several peculiarities. One was my reluctance to chew my food, as it was called. I swallowed what I ate whole, and made it easier by washing it down with milk. This wasn't allowed.

'Chew your food properly. Do as I say.'

I suppose they couldn't imagine that I actually had difficulty chewing. But I couldn't control my jaws all that well. I found it hard work to move at all, as I had to think out everything I did in order to be able to do it. In a way, I had to order my body to carry out what it had to do by thinking it out all the time. I had never been able to believe that I was meant to put so much labour into chewing my food when it was so easy just to swallow it whole. It seemed as absurd as if someone had said, whenever you needed fluid, that you should drink out of a glass while running. I thought if I was allowed to eat only what I liked, and if no one interfered, then everything would be all right. I wanted them to leave me alone.

But there were ways of dealing with problems of defiance and laziness. My father had his own method.

'Chew your food! Sit properly! Now just listen to me! Don't drink milk with every mouthful! Use your knife and fork! Listen to what I say, chew your food! Now just do as you're told! . . . You must learn some table manners. Chew your food before swallowing it . . . Do you hear what I say!'

Then there was my mother's method, mother's weary method.

'Leave the child alone . . .'

I didn't really understand what it was my father wanted me to do. Chew? How? I *am* chewing, aren't I?

12

When I didn't understand, I didn't bother much about what the grown-ups said—not just as a matter of obedience, anyway. But I was miserable inside because they thought me spoilt and lazy, and I thought they were right.

As the grown-ups said, I probably had no sense of shame either. I could go on and on about something for any length of time, far beyond their capacity to maintain their standpoint. Partly because I had no natural brake inside me, once something had begun, as far as I was concerned it could go on for ever. I didn't suddenly tire, or stop to think, nor did any disturbing impulses emerge from inside me. My ability just to go on and never give up was also partly due to the fact that these situations were always about things I thought vital.

My tenacity, consisting mostly of the word *no*, had two sources: my lack of that inner brake combined with a potential for panic that could make me invincible. Quite simply, I couldn't afford to lose. No one around me seemed to have the slightest idea of what my needs were. So I was totally at the mercy of my own judgement in doing those vital things, so obviously important to me, and the reason for which no one else seemed to have any idea. My family and I did not live in the same world. We scarcely came from the same planet.

It was always called 'defiance'. And if it looked like defiance, it had to be defiance. They measured me according to the way they measured themselves. They started from the premise that I was the same as they were, and if I wasn't really like them, then I ought to be. I also quite definitely had to want to be like them. If they were the gold of creation, I was a copper coin. That was what their world was like, and that was what everyone's world seemed to be like.

But for me they were a kind of unit, a mother-father-big-sister unit, and I was another unit quite apart from them. My life just happened to run parallel to theirs—

otherwise, we had nothing in common. I couldn't help that. It was neither my wish nor my idea—it was simply the way it was. I knew nothing else. This didn't mean I was cold and empty inside. I just didn't know I ought to belong to them, or that I ought to love them.

It was none of my choosing, this not belonging to them. It was just that I didn't. I couldn't change it and I didn't know what a person was meant to be. Inside, I was miserable. Why did they always get so angry? Why didn't they understand?

Of course, I wanted to eat things that didn't need chewing in order to be swallowed, and I had no need for variety in my food. I just liked eating the same things all the time. Although my mother tried every imaginable way of persuading me to take other food, for long periods I ate nothing but skinless sausages and chocolate pudding. But then I would suddenly acquire a taste for something else. For a while when I was five I ate nothing but liver pâté and prunes, refusing everything else. As usual, the grown-ups could do very little about it.

I didn't find it dull eating the same thing all the time, though should it start to become so, that was nothing compared with the mortal danger of risking unknown food. My teeth were very sensitive, and inside my mouth the consistency of some foods could be unpleasant, giving me a horrible feeling all over. With unknown food, you never knew what might happen. So if sometimes it was boring eating only skinless sausages and chocolate pudding, it was definitely worth it.

They sometimes said things about food I didn't understand. This confused me and made me even less inclined to try anything unfamiliar. Then it was almost easier to understand when they were angry with me.

'Food doesn't bite you,' they said, laughing.

But what did they know about it?

The chewing surface of my teeth was occasionally

incredibly sensitive to touch—almost electric—and seemed to be connected to a sensitive place at the back of my neck. This could be unbearable, and it helped to bite into something—preferably something fairly resistant to the teeth—then the pressure in my mouth evened up. Human flesh was the very best of all to bite into. I wanted to put my teeth into someone, an arm. I didn't know why. I just felt I needed to.

I liked biting people, and on the odd occasion I was allowed to bite my big sister. But mostly I had to be content with things made of soft plastic—my old teething ring, toys, furniture . . . whenever I needed to calm that unpleasant feeling in my teeth, I bit into whatever was handy.

When I grew older, into my teens, I found I could ask people whether I might bite them. Strangely enough, I was often allowed to, even if it raised a few eyebrows. Some people actually let me bite their arms or hands for a moment, as long as I didn't hurt them.

My teeth seemed to be the part of my body where I had the best feeling. Outside my body, I experienced feeling more diffusely. Only vague information reached my mind when something or other happened; I needed to look at my body in order to know where I felt something. The further away from my head, the less the feeling. My feet were a white space on the map of my body. Although I otherwise found light touches difficult, the soles of my feet weren't ticklish as they are with so many other people. On the other surfaces of my body, light, soft touches tensed me, tightening the springs hard inside me and becoming unbearable. But under my feet that touch did not have the same effect. It was the only place where I could bear almost anything and actually like it, because I felt it so faintly. To be tickled with a piece of grass on my soles was the only little touch I could accept, the only little touch I experienced with feeling without being tormented by it.

In many areas I functioned in the opposite way to other children, while in others I was just like any other child. Certain things expected of me didn't function at all, and some were the opposite one day to the way they were the next. But things simply couldn't be like that; it all seemed totally inexplicable. And if something was inexplicable, then it was nonsense. I'd concocted it all, or I wanted to draw attention to myself. I was lazy and defiant—that must be it. My parents were certain, because they had the yardstick for human beings, the universal mould they knew every person had to be pressed into.

'So just stop that!'

Either they were angry with me, or they made fun of me at my expense. They often took a difficulty I had and turned it into an amusing little anecdote. They would take a deadly seriousness, my seriousness, and turn it into a great laugh that they would then let out into the room. What kind of people were they to do that? The amusing anecdote had sharp edges, flew into me and scratched my soul.

Rather their *anger*, then. A thousand times rather their *anger*.

My consolation, my safe retreat in the world, was a brown armchair in one corner. I could just fit in behind it. With my face close to the back of it, I would stare into the upholstery so that I could see every tiny little bit of it. I became absorbed in the brown material, in its threads, in the minute holes between the threads. Then the scratches on my soul would heal a little. I never turned to anyone for consolation. There was a self-consoling unit inside me, the only form of solace I knew, and that is where I went. I didn't know you were meant to get that from other people.

I never sucked my thumb or had a dummy. On the other hand, I often put my feet in my mouth. My body was so supple that I could fold it in almost every way. I used to sit on the floor—always the floor, for chairs weren't safe—either with my toes in my mouth or with my legs folded along my sides. When I stood up, I often put the whole of my hand in my mouth, sometimes with my other hand between my legs. This was a way of trying to press back the horrible thing creeping at the nape of my neck and down my spine. A way of trying to press it back from both directions, so that what was unpleasant couldn't grow and become bigger than me. At that point they always told me to go to the toilet. I didn't know why I should, because I didn't want to go. I tried to protest, but that was no good, because they were quite certain I wanted to.

I didn't like the grown-ups laughing. It seemed sudden and horrible to me, as if their faces were cracking, huge mouths, with no previous warning. Suddenly a lot of teeth and loud noises. Smiles were better; they were slower, although they could also make me uncertain.

'Don't laugh!' I thought I was expressing myself quite clearly, but they didn't seem to catch on.

'*Don't* laugh!' The greater my solemnity, the funnier it seemed to be.

'But dear, we're not laughing at you ... Hahaha ... come on, little one ... Hahaha ... don't take it all on yourself ... Hahaha.'

All I wanted was for them to stop laughing, but I couldn't find any way of making them. I said quite clearly what I wanted, but it was no use. I was being utterly serious, deadly serious, and they thought it was funny! I tried to understand what was happening, but I couldn't. I slipped in behind the brown armchair again and shut out everything except myself and the material.

I wanted to be left in peace there behind the armchair, and I often was. I just stayed there, just being, absorbed in the material on the back of it. There was no energy to be found there, but there was rest, a way of keeping my mouth shut and holding on to a little of the energy that had otherwise been spent in trying to understand what was incomprehensible, how everything hung together. But my father had no respect for my need to be left in peace. He had no respect for anyone's needs. He would lean over the armchair and, with no warning, grab hold of me and haul me out. He thought that was fun. Or—even more fun—he would suddenly move the armchair so that I was assailed by the room, the light and all those impressions. For him, I was an object. For him, everything he possessed was an object. Amusing things with which to entertain himself.

The effect of my father's actions was often one of pure sadism, although he wasn't really a sadist. He didn't enjoy my humiliation in itself—he couldn't even imagine it. He just thought quite simply that it was fun, and whatever I did looked funny. If animals or people were held tight and then wriggled to get free, or if they were shocked, frightened or struggling to reach something, their behaviour amused him. And I behaved in a way that amused him, while he offended *me*. In his eyes, my desire to be left alone was amusing, and the more I struggled the more amusing it was.

'The kid's got to learn to take a joke.'

He often told me what fun it had been to joke with my sister Kerstin when she was little. Kerstin couldn't crawl, but she hauled herself along on her backside instead. That meant she found it difficult to get over the little door-sills. My father thought it great fun to put a biscuit on the other side of the sill and watch her struggle to get over. He was amused by her suffering. Another favourite game of his was to press liver pâté on to the cat's nose and watch his contortions in his desire to get it into his mouth. The more desperate the cat got, the funnier my father thought it was.

My mother did make some efforts on my behalf. She saw that father's jokes tormented me, although she didn't really understand why.

'Can't you leave the kid alone . . .'

But my mother, also one of his objects, had no power over him. She occasionally tried to console me, but she found it difficult to accept that I was inconsolable. I had no sense of her having any idea of how I felt inside. Whenever she tried consoling me, a feeling of unreality came over me, as if I were being consoled for a graze on my nose when in fact I had broken both legs.

I didn't understand what she wanted when she spoke in that sickly kind of voice. 'There there . . .'

I thought she sounded peculiar and I didn't like that voice. So I tried simply ignoring her. On the whole, I didn't want her to come anywhere near me, especially with that voice; it was horrible and unfamiliar and somehow sort of runny.

As I grew older, I did occasionally sense her need to console me, and I realised that voice had something to do with it. Then I was sometimes able to let it conquer my need to be left alone, to pretend to be comforted for a while because *she* needed it, because it was simpler like that—endure this first and be left in peace afterwards. That was when I learnt that it was easiest to let it be 'what it wasn't'.

I spent a great deal of time inside myself, as if in my own world, screened off from everything else. But there was no world there inside me, nothing more than a kind of nothing layer, a neither-nor, a state of being hollow without being empty or filled without being full. It just was, in there, inside myself. This emptiness wasn't tormenting in itself. I was inside the emptiness and the emptiness was inside me—no more than that. It was nothing but a kind of extension of time—I was in that state and it just went on. But the sense of unreality and of always being wrong when I was out in the world, outside myself, was always harder to bear.

I often sat in the garden looking at something, absorbed in a flower or a leaf. Then I felt neither wrong nor right. I just was, and that never stopped. I never suddenly wanted to do something else. Nothing was happening there inside me. I sat looking, observing.

Very early on, I learnt to turn my observations into pictures, and I could be very creative in my solitude. My first human figure had eyes, nose and mouth, arms and legs. I was just two when I drew it. I noticed details, and my drawing quickly developed. I wanted to reproduce what I saw and thought it important to get everything in, absolutely everything: nostrils, eyebrows and the correct number of fingers and toes. When I started drawing houses, they too turned out like humans—the windows were the house's eyes and the door was the mouth. To me the difference between people and houses was not obvious.

I also very much liked doing things with small objects. I would cut out tiny bits of paper and stick them on to cardboard. I made little men out of wool. Whatever I created became increasingly smaller—I wanted to see how small it was possible to go. I liked it when it was fiddly and rather difficult to do, so that it took all my attention. I felt no particular need to show anyone what I had done, but I very much wanted to sell my products. I wanted my parents to buy the woolly men, and sometimes they did; twenty-five öre each I took for them. Money was good to have. I knew that.

I had no problem dealing with failing at something that I had decided to do on my own. I simply tried again until it worked. When I had set the goal myself, my patience was infinite. But when other people demanded something of me, I found it difficult that I failed so often. And every time it happened, I became even more sensitive and felt I was one great failure.

I had no means of knowing why I couldn't manage what was required of me. I often saw very clearly that others thought I ought to be able to manage it. What they wanted me to do often seemed absurd and unreasonable. On other occasions, I needed to try many more times than they had the patience to allow me.

I always felt there was something I didn't really understand. That feeling was constant and followed me everywhere. Even when I understood quite a lot, there was always something left—the actual way it all hung together. I thought and thought. I made a huge effort, and then an even greater effort. The world was an ever-changing mystery, things happening suddenly. How? Why?

Sometimes it was all so incomprehensible, I couldn't even find an end in the tangle to pull at. Then I would turn in on myself, knowing neither the question nor the answer; and I couldn't tell anyone. My state was just one colour inside myself. I was the only one who had colours: I had an internal colour system which became a way of connecting information about different worlds, about the nursery world and the garden world. Everything became a colour inside me—people, words, feelings, atmospheres. Not understanding was faintly orange, a pale orange with sunlight coming through it. Tiredness, what I hadn't the energy to try to understand, came and laid a dark green on top of the orange light and put it out.

The dining-room world, the kitchen world and the hall world—none of these had anything to do with each other until a colour made me connect. If my mother said something in a violet-coloured way in the kitchen and two months later used that violet tone of voice in the bathroom, I suddenly realised that the kitchen and the bathroom had something to do with each other, so I could begin to find other similarities such as that there was water in both rooms. But the first connection was always via colours.

It often helped to have all these colours connecting the different bits of life together, but sometimes it caused problems. I might have great difficulty letting go of the idea that two things belonged together because of the colours, although I hadn't found any other common denominator. Then great amounts of energy would go on trying to find something that would clarify the connection. Perhaps those things really did have nothing whatsoever to do with each other.

Kerstin was three years older, but despite that we had a language in common, a language which was not just words. She seemed to perceive the contours of what was really me and was able to function as a communication link between me and my parents. On the other hand, my parents seemed to see quite another child when they looked at me. Kerstin became a mouthpiece because she intuitively understood I wasn't like other small children, so the same things couldn't really be demanded of me as of others of my age.

Kerstin often answered for me when someone asked me a question. I sometimes thought that was good, but the older I grew the more troublesome it became that she put words into my mouth. Sometimes I could have answered perfectly well myself, only I needed time to shape the reply in my head and then say it. I often felt overrun when Kerstin, hurrying to cover up for her little sister, had already answered for me while I was still busy shaping my words. Kerstin and I were so different, and perhaps it was my slowness that made her accelerate. She raced through life, while I jogged along somewhere behind her.

I sometimes felt my mother wanted something of me, but I didn't realise what she wanted was my love. She seemed to want to take something from me, something it was vitally necessary for me to keep. If I *did* have some inkling of what she was after, her idea of how it should be expressed was totally incomprehensible to me. That people should want to have other people's feelings, want to force them out, seemed to me just as incredible as if they had wanted each other's internal organs. I thought my mother intruded on me.

What did she want of me? Why didn't she leave me alone? What *did* she want? I didn't understand. She wanted to take something from me. Go away! I want to be left alone! Why didn't she leave me in peace?

Go away! You've nothing to do with me!

I didn't think anyone had anything to do with me, especially not my parents. So neither did I think I had to obey them. If I had to take notice of what anyone said, it seemed more sensible to listen to my sister. She at least found it easier to get me to understand how and why. I thought it offensive that grown-ups not only decided things for me, but also thought they had the right to do so. I wanted to be left in peace, but I also wanted to be loved. I just didn't know how things were supposed to be. I wanted to be loved the way I was, and when that didn't happen it never occurred to me that you had to pay to be loved, as I realised later that others paid to be loved— with ingratiation or obedience, or some other kind of behaviour. If I couldn't be loved, then I wanted to be left alone.

I thought I had a right to be as I was, that I had a right to have my sense of integrity respected. I thought it was other people who were behaving so incomprehensibly and strangely, not me.

Two

I was four when my sister started school. It must have been discussed beforehand, and my mother presumably tried to prepare me for it. But talk about things I couldn't visualise never stuck in my head—it would just fly away and settle somewhere else. The words possibly stuck, but only as words, interesting in their structure or flavour. They might have exciting colours or contain pleasant sounds, but if I couldn't visualise them they meant nothing.

My mother and I were now left to ourselves in the day-time, totally without any common language. She had some kind of vague, indistinct language, filled with 'in a minute', 'maybe' and 'later', and mine was concrete and exact. I mostly didn't grasp what she meant, and she almost never understood that I meant just what I said. This resulted in my sometimes having violent outbursts of temper and throwing things about. When I didn't have these outbursts, I would go and sit behind furniture or get under beds. I would pick at the material with my nails, liking the feel of the rough surface. I also liked being in small cramped spaces where it was quiet and calm, especially when I fitted exactly into the space. I wanted to put on a space, put on a sort of cave, like a garment—it felt safe when it was cramped. There were to be no gaps between things, and when I fitted into something exactly, a calm came over me. That calm could quieten the uneasy feeling I always had at the nape of my neck.

I felt the same calm when something fitted exactly into something else; then I could take them apart and put them together over and over again, just to feel the satisfaction of their fitting so well. But there were times when something was only nearly right, and that disturbed me. Like those Russian dolls that had another old woman inside them. The proportions between the larger and smaller ones were always the same, except for the last doll, which didn't fit as well into the next-but-last one. It was tiny and rattled about inside. Then it was all wrong. I was annoyed, but when I was disturbed by such details, I was also confused. I kept on thinking: how could this be? Had the maker of the dolls made a mistake? Perhaps some dolls that should have been in between the next-but-last and the last one were missing? I wondered how I could find out how many there ought to be. I was aware that a lot of people knew about Russian dolls—so, in other words, perhaps it was known from the outset how many dolls a Russian doll should have inside it? That ought to be so—otherwise, how would the doll-maker know? I searched for differences in the last doll that would tell me why it was proportionately smaller than the others. Perhaps it was a child doll? But it had exactly the same shawl and the same old-woman appearance as all the others. This was confusing, and I simply couldn't let go of things in which I could find no order. For years I kept thinking about the situation of those Russian dolls.

My mother tried to deal with my outbursts. When I threw china around, I was given my own box of old chipped cups and plates and would go out and smash them on the stone steps. This probably had no direct effect on my tantrums, but I was pleased to be allowed to throw things about without anyone being angry. And I liked the sound when they broke.

But my mother couldn't really cope, and she was also frightened of me. She called them 'furious temper tantrums', but to me they had nothing to do with rage, but more with a strong sense of panic. Although my mother could often see no reason at all for these outbursts, for me it was always something immensely important, a matter of life and death. Sometimes it would be triggered by something that had happened a long time before and that I linked with something happening now. It could be something suddenly connecting inside me and producing painful consequences. I would be miserable, despairing or panic-stricken, because I had suddenly realised this something, while my mother thought nothing had happened that could be a motive for my behaviour.

If anyone then tried to take hold of me or come anywhere near me, I felt threatened. No! Don't come here. You mustn't come here. I've decided. Go away!

I knew my mother couldn't cope, and I thought that was perfectly all right. I made the decisions about myself, and she ought not to interfere. That was just as it should be. But I also vaguely understood that I made her feel a failure. I didn't really grasp it, but I saw the colour of her feeling of not knowing how to deal with me. I felt I was the cause of something disagreeable.

I didn't understand why my sister had suddenly disappeared in the daytime. Kerstin had always been there before, and now she no longer was. As my visual impressions were very clear and sharp, I connected whatever happened with what I could see. To me, everything boiled down to what I saw, and sight was the most reliable of my senses. It was as if my sight was tangible.

I desperately wanted to understand, and this led to theories: if everything looked in a certain way in the living-room—the sun shining in through the curtains, the ash-tray on the table with a newspaper beside it—and if Kerstin then came back from school . . . I thought that everything had to look exactly the same the next day, for her to come back from school. It quite simply had to be like that. And in fact, it often was.

Of course, there were sometimes exceptions that made

me doubt my theory. That doubt was a painful feeling, and I wanted to understand. I was a mental marionette hanging on strings of theories. When the theories didn't fit and I could find nothing new to hang on, I was unable to move mentally. So I had to create new theories all the time.

People often disturbed my theories. Just when I thought I had grasped the connection between things, someone moved the newspaper and I no longer knew what to think. Would Kerstin not come home now? Couldn't she come home? Ever again? Or didn't I understand anything? In that case, was everything else I thought also quite wrong? No, it must be that my sister couldn't come home until everything was put right again. The newspaper had to be back in its place—that must be it. If it wasn't like that, everything I believed in and knew about was invalid.

There was no flash of magical thinking in all of this. On the contrary, it was all immensely concrete—what I saw was what happened, neither more nor less. On these occasions when my theory was sabotaged by things not turning out as I'd anticipated, I had to start on a new one. There had to be *some* way of understanding the world.

Strangely enough, my theories quite often fitted, although naturally they were entirely wrong. Later on when I was adolescent, and then adult, this ability to link situations with visual impressions, or arrange them inside my internal colour system, led to my being able to discover connections long before I saw them—though without being able to explain them. So, of course, in the world of school they became invalid.

Occasionally, I lost all sense of perspective. Something would seem monstrously large if coming towards me at speed, or if I was unprepared. Someone suddenly leaning over me could frighten me enormously. I felt something was falling on to me and that I'd be crushed underneath it. I didn't run away or throw myself to one side. The panic was all inside. Help! I'll be squashed. Where am I? Where is my body? What's up and what's down?

Inside, I rescued myself. I gathered up everything that was me, stuffed it inside and closed the door. That was the quickest way of surviving the situation. I hadn't understood that one should show one's feelings on the outside. Showing my terror would also have required energy— energy I couldn't afford to waste. When I actually did show how frightened I was, whatever it was didn't seem to frighten anyone else, and what frightened other people didn't worry me in the least.

I was unable to have my feelings confirmed anywhere, so I presumed the others were right. I must be silly, wilful, stubborn, rude, lazy and spoilt. But inside, deep down, I did not accept their truths. I knew that when I was afraid, I was afraid, and nothing else. I lived with two opposing truths; and in time I got so used to it, I thought that was as it should be. I thought a feeling wasn't real if it didn't contain two opposing truths. If the surrounding world did not confirm that reality conflicted with my innermost conviction, in the end I found it difficult to feel I existed at all.

To them it was silliness, defiance and peculiarities. But certain sounds frightened me—dogs barking, mopeds, tractors and cars, engines of various kinds. They would explode inside me and make me lose all sense of the way my body related to my surroundings. It was like being flung out into space. Straight out into space—whoosh— quite without warning. Sometimes I screamed and covered my ears, and my mother was embarrassed when I behaved oddly.

Those years when my sister went to school and I was at home with my mother, she was probably the person to see most of my strange behaviour. I would go shopping with her, to the post office and the wine store on Fridays.

It was hard work for me to walk far, although I was considered too big to be in a pram. The world that decided how long it was appropriate for children to be in prams had no regard for the fact that I had to think 'I am walking' in order to be able to walk, step by step. The omnipotent world around me didn't know about that—so it didn't count.

But I refused to walk, and my mother had no means of objecting. She knew my refusal meant refusal, and that there could be no negotiating. So the pram was brought out and she had to put up with people wondering why such a large child was in a pram. Some of her embarrassment was probably due to the fact that she felt weak in her relationship with me, that she was ashamed not to be able to manage such a simple thing as deciding for her child. Perhaps she thought I behaved in such a strange way only with her, that it was her lack of skill as a mother that produced my difficulties. For when the whole family was out in the car, I sat quite calmly and quietly in the back, singing at length about what I could see out of the window.

My father was the one who had a driving licence, so it was he who had the power to move about freely. He owned my mother and the means of transport, as well as his children. He never walked anywhere and always went by car. He smoked sixty cigarettes a day, and took the car down the hill whenever he wanted to buy some. He was often away somewhere—at work, it was said. And when he happened to be at home, the family was there for him. Then we were all to be together and do as he wanted.

When the whole family did things together, we always went by car. I liked that, and when I was inside the car the sound of the engine did not affect my nervous system. Then it was bearable, even pleasant. I sat in my allotted place in the back and sang. I had to sing in the car— quite simply, it was essential. That was why I liked going in the car so much, because the buzzing sound in the background helped me sing about what I could see.

My father didn't like me singing and told me to stop. But the only time I had any direct link between impressions and voice was precisely when I was singing my monotonous strings of words. And it was a strong feeling that I experienced in myself, there in the back of the car, the feeling that my voice could give words to what I saw without my having to stop at the thinking stage, find words for it, then send them on for my voice to sing. So it made me very miserable when they told me to be quiet. I tried taking no notice of them, but then they got angry. Everything was so strange and incomprehensible. They knew I loved going in the car, so they told me that I could ride in the car if I promised not to sing, that I could be in the car only if I kept quiet. But I liked going in the car just to be able to sing. How was I to understand what they meant? I became very confused.

I made sounds in those pre-school years—sniffing and grunting noises—whenever I was doing things. If I was drawing, I might sniff at regular intervals; when I was in bed I would make grunting noises before falling asleep. The sounds most often came when I felt all was calm and quiet. I never noticed them myself, but they often disturbed those around me. Other children, Kerstin's friends, found them annoying, and at first I didn't understand why they kept telling me to be quiet. I hadn't said anything, had I? The sniffing and snoring noises were as unconscious an accompaniment to what I was doing as was the beat of my heart. I simply didn't hear them.

As I grew older, I realised I was making noises the moment someone told me to stop, and I'd make an effort to stop, but after a while I unconsciously drifted back into making them. They were only there because they needed to be there, perhaps helping me to keep going in the same way as the engine noise in the car made my nervous system wake up and function better.

Some sounds around me I hardly reacted to at all. And there were others, louder ones, that I never even heard, or never seemed to hear—perhaps they were slopping about somehow in my ear without actually going inside. I hadn't the energy to sit there keeping guard over my ear all the time, to catch any possible sounds. When I did happen to have a scrap of energy left, then I was able to catch even the sounds that tended to stop half-way and carry me with them to my brain for further investigation. The result was that what I heard one day, I perhaps didn't hear the next.

However, I always heard whispers. But that couldn't be right—you can't hear one thing and be deaf to another. They knew what people were like, so I had to be good and adapt myself accordingly. It was just another of my tricks, saying that I couldn't hear. I was just making it up. So they were right, of course, to scold me for my silliness.

'She just hears what she wants to hear. Damned brat!'

Whenever they spoke to me, or called to me, I would be sitting on the floor. But I didn't hear them. I was absorbed in what I was doing and heard nothing, cutting up tiny bits of paper, totally concentrating on what I was doing. I had a large piece of paper on to which I was taping smaller pieces in a lovely pattern. I heard nothing. But they said it wasn't true that I couldn't hear. I wasn't listening, that was it. After all, if they whispered, I could hear.

But whispers came rushing at me from a long way off, always straight into my head, easily passing through all the passages in my ears, sliding directly up into my mind and rousing it. I didn't have to be on guard for whispers. I didn't have to wait to let them in. Whispers had their own key. So if people whispered when I was cutting out my little bits of paper, I looked up. *Then* I heard them.

But according to the prevailing adult logic—if a person said she couldn't possibly eat *anything*, then she certainly couldn't eat any dessert—I couldn't possibly, of course, hear only sometimes. They had never heard of any such thing. And if you'd never heard of any such thing, it didn't exist. If I heard whispering through several rooms, then I could certainly hear when someone stood right beside me, speaking to me. And if I didn't answer, then it was defiance. That was that.

Naturally, they were able to make fun of this characteristic, and naturally they could make fun of me. This was, after all, my own trick and my own fault, and as you make your bed so must you lie on it. So my mother thought up an 'It's all your fault' game, clearly a kind of bullying, but justified by the fact that it was all my fault. She didn't usually joke much, but now Kerstin had a chance to share something funny with her. They became allies in the game. It began by their calling out to me, and my not hearing them. Then my mother and sister would stand on the stairs whispering something about a bar of chocolate, or an ice-cream or a bag of sweets. I would hear their whispers, and want some too—I liked sweets a lot. But when I went to them, they just laughed. What they had been whispering about wasn't true, there were no sweets. I had gone there unnecessarily. I was bewildered.

The next day, they might stand outside my room and whisper about buns. I would feel just like a bun, and go out to them. I wanted a bun, too. But it would turn out that they'd just invented it, and there were no buns. I couldn't make it out at all. Then they would laugh. They thought they had found an amusing way of attracting my attention. As they had kept on calling out and I hadn't answered, it was my fault. It must have been I who had driven them to make fun of me in that way.

I didn't hear them calling, and I fell for it over and over again. I was incapable of linking the one event with the other. There was nothing inside me signalling that what was happening was exactly the same as the last time, and as that had been a lie, then it was sure to be a lie this time too. No warning signals lit up inside me.

Each time I thought I was going to be given some sweets, but instead it turned out that I was to clean my teeth, or eat something or go and wash. Each time, I was equally disappointed. Incapable of linking the one situation with the other, I became increasingly distrustful when I noticed that there was something that didn't fit. I hadn't heard them calling out, only their whispers. I felt stupid and offended. What was it that other people seemed to know that I didn't?

When I was four, I wanted an accordion. They asked me what I wanted for my birthday and I replied.

'An accordion.'

They nodded, without implying in any way that that would be an impossible birthday present.

I never wished for toys—I usually didn't know what they were for. I thought they were childish. I wanted real things. I didn't think of toys as proper birthday presents. An accordion was the only thing I wanted for this birthday, and I thought I would be given one. I hadn't really understood that all that stuff about wishing for something only meant that you *might* be given it. I was convinced I would be given the accordion I so very much wanted.

On the morning of my birthday, I was woken up with the usual birthday song and a tray of cocoa and sandwiches, summer flowers in a vase on my bedside table and parcels spread out on my bed. I was aching for the accordion— I preferred pre-arranged presents to surprises. What was sometimes difficult about some presents and surprises was that peculiar feeling of expectation, which I never could make out. I didn't know how I ought to be, but I was nearly always wrong, so other people were disappointed in me. Not only was I scared of surprises, but I was also made to endure my own terror of them. And it was also wrong of me to be scared. I oughtn't to have been scared—I ought to have been happy. So I liked presents most of all when I knew what was in them.

I opened all the presents lying on my bed, but there was no accordion. However, in one of the parcels was a hideous little object in blue plastic. This, they said, was an accordion.

'Just what you wanted,' they said. I was confused and dismayed. I didn't understand.

This couldn't be an accordion. This was something small, ugly and pale blue. I'd seen accordions, after all. They were beautiful, dark red and gleaming, with rows of white buttons. Shiny, and with a lovely sound inside them. But they showed me that this thing was an accordion, that you could play on it. It said toot when you pulled it out and the same toot when you pushed it back. How could they say this was an accordion? It had none of the characteristics I associated with an accordion.

The pleating of the bellows was the only thing this object had in common with a real accordion. The actual bellows, though, and the pulling in and out, were absolutely not what I saw as characteristic of an accordion. I hadn't even noticed that. So it was no accordion to me. This blue thing must be something quite different—anyone could see that. This thing was neither big, red nor shiny. It hadn't many buttons and it didn't sound nice. And yet they said it was an accordion—were they trying to deceive me?

It was something to do with language. I felt inside me that I had a grasp of language, and yet it didn't work. If I said 'an accordion', I thought they would understand I meant 'an accordion'. It couldn't be said in any other way—an accordion is an accordion. Surely I didn't have to say everything an accordion *isn't*? That seemed quite crazy.

34

An accordion is not a blue plastic object, an accordion is not . . . But no, you just couldn't say things like that.

There was something strange about their language. I would say exactly what I meant, but then it would become something else. The older I grew, the more often I had the feeling that when I said exactly what I meant, loud and clear, other people seemed to hear something else. And when I heard exactly what *they* said, it turned out that they had meant something else. I always said exactly what I meant, neither more nor less. That other people didn't do that was very confusing. They couldn't understand my disappointment, and I had no words with which to explain it to them. They pulled out the plastic thing, toot, toot, and wanted me to be pleased. All I knew was that everything about it was wrong, but I couldn't say in what ways.

The feeling of things being *wrong* had to come out somehow. Usually, the way in which it did was utterly incomprehensible and inappropriate to them. I threw aside the ugly things I didn't want. And if I hadn't the strength to do that, I would search around for a place in which to concentrate on consoling myself. I never sought out anyone else. It wasn't really that I evaded seeking consolation with someone else, but that it just never occurred to me that that was even possible.

Three

I loved cranes. They were one of my great passions. It made me happy just to look at them. When I was taken to a new place, which I usually disliked because new places were so unpredictable, I could be made to accept it if it was possible to see cranes from the window. This was a familiar starting-point, as I could see cranes from the nursery window at home. With at least one safety point, I could cope with trying to take in everything else new. People were never safety points to me.

I was convinced that cranes were alive. I could see from my window that they had moved their heads during the night. I thought that people used them in the daytime and then they were able to live freely at night. But when I told the grown-ups that they moved at night, they said I was imagining things, that it was only a fantasy, one of my fabrications. But I saw that the cranes had moved during the night and I tried to talk about it with deep seriousness. They laughed and said oh, what an imagination I had. Haha.

Many years later, when I was twenty-four, I met a construction engineer who told me that they disengaged the cranes in the evening so that they could swing in the wind. So cranes did actually move at night. Haha. But that haha never healed me. It merely settled like a membrane over the wound. There was nothing there to triumph over.

Other creatures also caught my interest. Earthworms were one of my great delights and I developed a similar passion for them. I fondled them and kissed them. I dug them up in the garden and cautiously patted them.

My mother did not approve of my love of worms and wanted me to be less intimate with them. One day she sat with me in the garden and tried to explain that I didn't have to kiss them, that patting would be enough. As I didn't understand why I shouldn't kiss them, I took no notice of what she said. Then my mother made a good decision—the family should buy a cat. It worked. I loved our cat, whom we named Knatte. Love in the cat way, a love with one's integrity maintained, suited me very well. Knatte received more of my kisses, the worms fewer, and my mother was satisfied, for it was more acceptable to fondle a cat. That didn't seem at all unhealthy.

Kerstin was one of the good things in my life. I could play with her, although otherwise I found it difficult to play with children. I had no clear grasp, even, of the fact that other children existed. Kerstin was older than me, and could guide me a little at play as well as in the world. I could sometimes use her as a model. Out there in the world, I was always half a step behind her and trying to do what she did, and in that way I often succeeded in fitting in a little better. Sometimes I really did walk just behind her and did exactly what she did. I had no idea how strange this looked, or why she would get so cross with me.

Kerstin could decide on which games to play as well as what I was to do in a way that suited me. I thought it was fun. She could also show a little forgiveness when I kept on wanting to do the same thing. My mother and father thought I was tedious and disagreeable, and told me I didn't know when to stop. They said I was the kind who, if you gave them a little finger, would take the whole hand.

I often wanted to do the same thing over and over again, and I could never have enough. Kerstin must sometimes also have thought I was rather trying, but she managed to rise above this feeling because she sensed that I wanted to do it so very much. I liked playing rather empty and mechanical games best. Sometimes Kerstin's patience ran out and I had to pay her for playing cars with me, for instance. In this game, we would lie at each end of a sofa with the soles of our feet pressed against each other, shouting 'Vrooom vrooom'. It could cost five or ten öre to be allowed to play cars with her, and I had to steal the money from my parents' piggy-bank. I didn't mind doing that at all.

Another of those mechanical, always-the-same games was one in which Kerstin would lie on her back with her knees drawn up and I would hang over her with her knees against my stomach and try just to brush against her nose. I liked the game because it was safe. I knew the rules and I understood the outcome. But I also liked it because it contained just the amount of physical contact that I could cope with—an even pressure against a large area of my body. We couldn't play it the other way round, with me below, because a light touch of the kind involved in that position was unbearable to me.

To be just lightly touched appeared to make my nervous system whimper, as if the nerve ends were curling up. If anyone hit on the terrible idea of tickling me, I died. It was so way beyond unbearable unbearableness that I simply *died*—or that's what it felt like. Now and again, it did happen that when I fell into the hands of other children I was tickled. The insane panic I showed seemed to frighten them, but it also seemed to spur them on. Kerstin, too, knew how to make use of my terror, of course. If she thought I was being a nuisance and wanted to be rid of me, she only had to hold out a hand and tickle the air a little for me to flee in panic.

Kerstin was best of all at establishing contact with me— contact that I also wanted. Although she often considered me stupid and annoying, and although she wanted to be my mother and improve me, I did feel she liked me as I was. Also, at least when it was just her and me, that she didn't make so many comparisons with the way I *ought* to be.

When she and I were playing on our own, she often steered it all by 'telling' the game while we were playing it. She was able to invent fantastic jungles in my room and tell me who I was and who she was. The game amounted to the actual construction of our surroundings. With bed-clothes, chairs and her imagination, she built and told the story.

'This is a jungle and that's a tiger and you're a little girl who's got lost . . .'

I listened. I sat there and was what she told me I was. To my sister I *was* the lost child, so I could play. Sometimes, following her instructions, I might help build, but usually I was the one to fetch the building materials from various rooms in the house. I was quite satisfied with this division of roles and regarded our games as mutual exchanges. But when the building was finished, the game was over. I was not the sort of playmate who could go on spinning the yarn and playing in the jungle once it was finished. So Kerstin was the only child I could play with. She knew how to. She had found a way of playing with me that also gave *her* something.

Playing was for me the same as making things, and as we both liked drawing, Kerstin and I often drew together. She decided what we were to draw, and then we each drew it. She decided, and I carried it out. That was a way of being together that worked. It wasn't equal, but it contained a kind of mutuality that I found difficult to achieve with anyone else. The great differences between us were noticeable when we weren't together. When Kerstin played with her friends, I was alone. I was alone, by myself, but solitude in itself was no affliction because I was not interested in other children. I did not feel lonely. And yet it was hard not having any friends.

When my sister was to go to a party, I wanted to go,

too. But I didn't realise that parties were a result of having friends and that you had friends by playing with other children. It wasn't contact with other children that I missed, but parties meant cream-cake. I also wanted some cream-cake. I wanted to go to parties and be given a bag of sweets like the one Kerstin brought back with her. Why wasn't I given one?

I had inconsolable outbursts. I would throw things about and tear up paper. I screamed and bit and kicked and no one could help me. No one could explain why everything was so unfair, why I didn't fit in, why I didn't get bags of sweets. No one could explain why there was so much I didn't understand.

Kerstin would go to parties with a guilty conscience and try to bring back a bag of sweets for me. I stayed at home and didn't understand why she could go and I couldn't. I stayed at home and was the ugly duckling who never became a swan. I stayed at home and was Spot, the spotted rabbit in the family of white rabbits, the one that couldn't be shown to Grandfather. I stayed at home and was the changeling. But the fact was that I didn't have the wrong beak, nor did I have any spots, nor dark hair or brown troll eyes—nothing peculiar, nothing that was visible to anyone looking at me. I looked like any other child, and I tried and tried to be any other child, but it didn't work. I had to stay at home and be different.

On my birthdays, when I was to have a party, children seldom came because I didn't know any. Those who did come were perhaps some of my sister's friends and their younger brothers and sisters, but otherwise only adult relatives came. I didn't like the children who came on my birthdays. My mother had invited them—with some misdirected benevolence she thought there should be children at *my* birthday party as well. Perhaps she thought I would feel less lonely then, but instead I was offended. I couldn't understand why those children should be in my house, in my garden, on my birthday, playing with each other. I couldn't take part in their games. Three or four children were enough for it to become an indistinguishable confusion of arms and legs, voices and laughter. They frightened me and wore me out. It was like being in a room full of little rubber balls in constant movement. I would sit on my own somewhere, eating sweets, or detaching myself from the system, pulling out the plug and sinking into myself.

When I grew older, as I couldn't be with children I occasionally tried to be with adults.

'Run away and play,' they said.

But I could neither run nor play.

'Run away and play,' they said, as if I was any other child. So I tried to be any other child. But however hard I tried, it always struck a false note or produced a bitter taste. No 'any other child' appeared, only me pretending to be any other child. I sensed the difference. Oh, *how* I sensed the difference, screeching like chalk against a blackboard inside me. I saw it in the light thrown back from my reflection in the mirror, in the pupils of those around me. Like one of those mirrors in the fairground hall of mirrors—not genuine, not like others, not real. The child trying to be any other child, I heard the difference in the breeze that followed their voices when they answered. The difference screamed at me: you can't—however much you try, you'll be a poor copy of that child, any other child. But my creative tenacity was unfaltering. I tried and tried and tried. I tried much harder than I really had the energy for. I made such an effort to be another child, an ordinary child—a Kerstin child—any other child. I wanted to so very much.

One day my sister was playing with a friend at being the Virgin Mary, Joseph and the infant Jesus. I saw that my parents thought it was all terribly sweet. They cried out with delight about how charming it was. I stored that in my memory, and in my striving to do what ordinary children do, I tried to do the same. I wrapped myself up in a bedspread, put a doll in the newspaper basket and sat down to wait for my mother or father to pass by. I waited and waited. I didn't play with the doll, as I didn't know how to. My patience was endless. I just sat there, waiting to be found and be given a share of the delighted cries my sister had received a week or so earlier. When my mother finally looked into my room, so that she would understand I pointed at the doll and said: 'It's the infant Jesus.' How else would she know that she had to cry out how sweet and charming it all was, as she had done when Kerstin had played that game?

But she just laughed. She thought my crass comment was terribly funny and laughed. But I didn't want her to laugh. I didn't want to be funny. I wanted to be like my sister, by doing what she did. I had wanted her to look at me in the same way, and now everything had gone wrong. However great an effort I made, it simply didn't work. It always went wrong. Yet again, I had failed at being a child and a human being. That failure was a gigantic feeling for me to bear, a feeling far too great for my four-year-old body to contain, and it overflowed.

My outburst was totally incomprehensible to them. In their world, as they saw it, for no reason I suddenly became withdrawn and started throwing things about. In their world my feelings had no validity.

I was four and a half when my father moved out and the upper floor of our house was rented out to a Finnish couple. The furniture was taken down to the ground floor and suddenly I was to sleep in another room. The fact that my father had vanished meant nothing to me. I never asked after him, not once, and I never wondered where he had gone. I didn't know that you were expected to have fathers all your life. His disappearance was no odder to me than that one evening there could be a bowl of fruit on the kitchen table before I went to bed and that the next day, when I woke, it was no longer there. It was the same with my father: one day I had one and the next day I hadn't. I never gave it a thought. On the other hand, it greatly disturbed me when they moved the furniture. I didn't want to sleep in a new place. I wanted to be where I was used to being. You never knew what the consequences would be when they started moving things, so I wanted everything to be as it had always been. I thought that other things, things I connected with certain rooms and certain furniture, would also be changed, and this made me feel terribly unsafe.

My mother found it useful that I didn't ask after my father, for then she could avoid having to lie to me. To Kerstin, who naturally asked, she said that he had gone away on business. In reality, he had moved in with another woman. My mother didn't give much thought to the fact that it was rather odd that I didn't miss my father, as she had plenty to do trying to get him back. She put all her energies into getting him back. He meant more to her than anything else in her life, and she couldn't live without their mutually destructive contempt. Eventually, she managed to get him to leave his new love. He moved back home again six months later, and the Finnish couple moved out. I was confused and angry when I saw him again. This new father who had moved in looked so familiar. I didn't understand that it was the same one I had had six months earlier. I thought he was a new father. That he happened to look the same as the old one was of no significance. I didn't know that people couldn't look identical.

I had no sense of what my parents were really like. I hadn't the slightest idea that you were expected to have only one couple of parents who were to last all your life. Inside me, there was no insight that told me that it was so. I thought that you could just as well have several lots of parents and that they could be interchanged. Mother and father really had nothing to do with me and I didn't know what they were for, or what was the point of them at all. Nor did I know what distinguished my parents from any other adult men and women.

I had no need to possess my parents, and definitely did not think they owned me. I never said things, like other children with that right of possession in their voices, such as 'That's *my* mother.' And every time I was left where there was both a man and a woman, I thought they were my new father and mother. If I was left somewhere, I believed I was to live there for the rest of my life. The feeling it aroused in me could be panic, but often all I felt was a simple acceptance of the world order that I thought prevailed. A kind of Ah, yes. I didn't think this was good, so it was definitely not a matter of wishful thinking. But as no inner sense gave me any hint of how this business of mothers and fathers hung together, I had to fall back on my own ability to think. I thought I had worked out just how things were—that life was often awful and that I was seldom able to do anything about it. I often protested violently against being left anywhere, but once I was there with the new mother and father, I just tried to adapt to the situation, however difficult that might seem.

I thought I had no choice. Screaming didn't seem to help, as I would be left anyway. When my confusion became so great that I had neither time nor energy to show my feelings outwardly, to scream, fuss and fight, then I tried simply to survive.

One Easter, my sister and I were left with my father's mother and father. I had met my grandmother and grandfather before, but now I didn't know who they were, nor that they had anything to do with me. I didn't recognise them. I fought, wept, screamed, bit and kicked. I wanted to get away. I thought I was going to be left there for ever. I couldn't connect with any previous experience of being left and actually brought back home. Each situation was new and unique and had nothing to do with any previous one.

I screamed and screamed and Kerstin sat with me in bed half the night, cutting traffic lights out of cardboard, the only way of calming me down. She cut—green, red and yellow, stop and go—clear signals with a clear message. I liked traffic lights and they had a calming effect. The next day, and the next and the next, I tried to take in these new circumstances. I couldn't grasp why my sister could seem so unmoved. How could she go out into that unknown garden and play with unknown children? I couldn't understand, when my terror was so great, how she could look as if this was like any other day. Bewilderment buzzed inside my head.

Mother? Father? Were these my new mother and father? How could they be so old? So wrinkled and thin-haired?

We had changed mother and father and house and everything, and Kerstin just went on playing, as if that was nothing. As if nothing had happened.

I couldn't make out why everything had to change. It was awful and strange that everything was suddenly different—smells, sounds, furniture. I tried to adapt. I tried to call them Mamma and Pappa, these new people. They looked a little strangely when I said 'Mamma and Pappa?', but they didn't stop me. They didn't tell me they weren't my mother and father. They didn't explain the connection to me.

I searched for new cramped spaces in this home, places I could make my own. I found a shoe-rack in the hall, hidden by a heavy curtain. I crept in there and switched off the world around me. I sat in peace among the shoes and began to get used to this house. But one day, my mother and father were standing there in the hall and I was lifted out of my refuge behind the curtain. They were now to take Kerstin and me home. I was shocked to see them again. I thought they had ceased to exist. Suddenly everything I had worked out and understood was turned upside down. It was as if someone had turned my mind upside down and shaken it. Nothing was in its right place. Logic now told me I was to have a new mother and father all over again, and that they just happened to resemble the ones I had had before.

But that wasn't quite right, and I couldn't get it to go together. We moved back to our old home. We were simply to pretend—it was as if this new home had never existed before. And I was never certain whether they really were the same parents I had had before, just because they looked like them. Perhaps a great many people could look alike?

Four

I often used to sit on the floor somewhere in our house, arranging the alphabet cards I kept in a white plastic bucket. Father had made the cards for Kerstin, cutting them out of cardboard and drawing the letters on them. He was good at this kind of thing, and now I had taken them over from my sister. I used to lay out the cards in patterns or arrange them in various ways, perhaps putting all the Es in one pile and the As in another. I loved those alphabet cards. They were so clean and clear, on white cardboard with red edges. But it disturbed me that there weren't equal numbers of each kind. I thought there ought to be just as many Xs as Ss, so that all the heaps became equally large. And just as many Ys as Es. I didn't know why the letters were in such unequal numbers.

My mother and father were now quarrelling increasingly often, but at first I took no notice. I couldn't make out what they were doing, so I would go on playing with my alphabet cards. But I did sometimes wonder why Kerstin became so odd. She was often uneasy, red patches appearing on her cheeks; and she seemed to move in a different way—jerkily. If my mother locked herself in the lavatory, Kerstin would run after her. I didn't understand why. They were all suddenly moving in a different way and I thought it was strange, but I didn't give much thought to the fact that they were shouting, as long as they weren't shouting at me. If there were too many violent movements in the room, it disturbed me, and I would collect up my cards, put them in the bucket and go into another room to carry on arranging them. There seemed to be no point in even trying to understand what they were up to. Something told me that of the various kinds of human anger, some had to be distinguished as those that simply couldn't be understood, however hard I tried. So I gave up and went into another room. I was unable to recognise those emotions, that kind of aggressiveness, in myself. What other people regarded as my anger was often pure terror, and I could see and understand terror in others. I could empathise with other people being frightened, feeling small, insulted or exposed, because I had felt all that, too.

But I didn't know what these squabbles were about. I would try to find ways of avoiding what was incomprehensible, and the most constructive thing I could think up for when people were angry was to go somewhere else. On the other hand, if they were angry with *me*, I was often unable to go into another room because they held on to me, stopped me. But I could also go somewhere else inside me. I could leave the room without leaving the room.

When I was older, I was sorry for Kerstin when she was upset like that. I didn't understand why she was so shaken, nor what seemed to be vibrating inside her, but I could see she was miserable and felt sorry for her. I thought she ought to ignore mother and father—why should she care about what they did? But she often wanted to mediate between them, or take my mother's side against my father. I couldn't make out why she interfered in what they were doing. When things were quite beyond my ability to comprehend, I would go away. But that didn't mean there were no feelings inside me. I liked my sister very much and suffered when she suffered, but it was all so incomprehensible and upsetting. And once I was in the other room with my alphabet cards, I had stepped into another world. Then, what was happening in the living-room didn't exist any longer. Once I couldn't see it, I thought it couldn't be going on in there. Leaving the room was somehow the same as getting them to stop quarrelling.

There was no automatic system inside me telling me that I should love my parents just because they were that— my parents. I retained the right to choose whom I would love. This seemed to me fairly practical. But Kerstin wanted something of me, needed me in some way. She wanted me to be like her, and that we two should worry about it together. As I grew older, a feeling in me also grew, a feeling that I ought to be different. And it became increasingly clear: that feeling told me that I ought to react in just the same way as my sister reacted, that my way was wrong and peculiar. Obviously, it didn't matter that Kerstin's way was impractical and against all inner logic—it was the right way, anyway. Something must be missing inside me, and I was probably horrible for not loving my mother. Or was it perhaps because I was lazy, stupid, insufferable? I ought to mind about her, and I also ought to have red patches on my cheeks and knock on the lavatory door when she was crying. I wondered whether I could learn to understand *when* I should react in that way. Perhaps I ought to have practised and trained at it? But the feeling also told me that I should react as a matter of course. As a matter of course—that was difficult. I didn't know how that happened. Nothing was ever a matter of course to me.

When I woke, it was the middle of the night. I was five. I didn't know what had woken me. I felt slightly panicky as I always did when I woke in the night, because it was pitch-dark all around me. There was a little lamp on in my room, but that wasn't enough. I really liked sleeping with all the lights on, but I wasn't allowed to. I wanted to escape the feeling of being blind, a feeling I always had when things weren't properly lit. My eyes couldn't adjust to darkness. The others said I was afraid of the dark, but what I was afraid of was the feeling of being blind. Not the dark.

49

I had to feel my way through the room to open the door into the passage outside, where the light was on. When I came out, I heard sounds and voices from my parents' bedroom. The door into their room was open. I stood in the doorway and saw my father with his back to me on one side of the double bed, my mother on the other side. She was trying to get away from him. In one hand my father held a brass candlestick, the one that usually stood on the dining-room table downstairs. He went for my mother, got hold of her, wrestled her down on the bed, then hit her on the head with the candlestick. Blood appeared, bright-red blood. This was the first time I had seen them fighting and I wondered what they were doing. It looked peculiar. Why were they going on like this? I couldn't make it out.

Suddenly a pair of hands covered my eyes. It was Kerstin. She had woken up, too, and was now preventing me from seeing. She led me back to my room and told me I must go back to bed. She said I wasn't to be afraid or sad any longer, and that no harm was being done. The way she was and the way she was talking confused me even more. I was neither sad nor afraid, so why was she telling me not to be? Why wasn't I permitted to look? I wanted to know what it was they were doing that I didn't understand. They had appeared to be dancing around the bed and it had looked so strange, I wondered why they were doing it.

The next morning, my mother was sitting at the table when I came downstairs. This was different. She never usually sat there in the mornings, but would be busy clattering about in the kitchen. She never used to sit down. But now she was sitting there with a large cup of coffee in front of her. She was wearing sunglasses and there was a thick brown line over one eyebrow with dried blood all around it. She said something, trying to sound as usual, but her voice as she spoke had a red colour, a pale-red falsetto. And when she noticed me looking at the blood, she said that she had fallen downstairs the evening before and hit her forehead. The world was now totally incomprehensible, totally perplexing.

How could I possibly understand? Why was she telling it 'as it wasn't'? I had seen. I tried to think and think, but I couldn't make it out. My head grew very tired.

I learnt to recognise that bright-red streak in her voice. I didn't really know what it meant, but it often coincided with my mother wearing sunglasses. I wondered what the connection was—red voice and sunglasses. I couldn't fathom it, or the motive behind my parents' actions. I hadn't even grasped that there could be different motives behind the same action, so my mother telling a lie was totally bewildering to me. Her lie was telling it 'as it wasn't'. But I couldn't think 'Why doesn't she say it as it is?'—that would be going too far. I could only think 'Why does she tell it as it isn't?' This was the concrete way I related to lies.

It was a turning-point for me, to realise you could say things differently from the way they really were. Here was a tool to use in order to be more like other children and to get myself out of awkward situations. Saying it as it wasn't became synonymous with saying what the adults wanted to hear. The older I got, the more I learnt to make use of this technique. But not even when I thought I knew what a lie was did I consider I was lying when I said it as it wasn't. I wasn't lying. I was trying to survive. *Force majeure*—in such circumstances it couldn't be counted as a lie.

At times this technique could be a great help, and people seemed to get on better with me when I didn't say exactly how things were. But in the long run, it made me lose touch with my own identity. In the end I had said it as it wasn't so many times that I began to forget how it actually was. I believed in what I'd said, and all that was left was a vague sense of something not being quite right.

I was very clever at learning long pieces of text by heart. I didn't especially practise at it, but the words just stuck. They settled as a rhythm somewhere in my mind, and once I got hold of the first word of a piece I had heard, then the whole word-snake uncoiled and came out through my mouth. The words came all by themselves, and, as with other things, I never had to search for some place in my mind to put them.

I knew all my children's books off by heart, and I thought that meant I could read. I had seen Kerstin reading, slowly, with concentration, running her finger along the lines. So I did the same. I was 'reading'. I concentrated on the book and said what was there. I said it out loud and verbatim, but in the same hesitant tone of voice my sister used. I thought that was how it should sound when you were reading. As I knew all the pages in my books, I also knew exactly when I should turn over. My parents couldn't imagine that I actually *knew* all these texts, and they thought that at the age of five I had already learnt to read. I thought so too, and I was proud of it. I had known all the letters of the alphabet for a long time and was able to write simple combinations, so now I thought I had conquered the whole secret of literacy.

It was one of my aunts who took my delight in that away from me. My new skill was to be shown off to a gathering of relatives, and my aunt fetched a book in large print that I was to read. It was a book with frogs on the cover. I was lifted up on to a small table so that I could be seen properly. I opened the green frog book, but I didn't know what was there, because I had never seen the book before. I couldn't read it. My aunt was annoyed with me and said I was deceitful. Crossly, she lifted me down from the table. I had no idea what was happening. Why was she suddenly so angry? Why couldn't I read this book? One moment I'd been clever and attracting attention, then the next moment I was stupid and a liar. How could this be? All I could deduce was that yet again I had displeased the grown-ups. I was left with no explanations, and instead they went on to listen to my sister playing the recorder.

Fairly soon after this, I did learn to read after all. I learnt on my own with the alphabet cards and my powers of deduction. First of all I learnt to write, which was easier, and then I learnt to read. I liked words, and needed new challenges for it to be fun. I wanted to learn more and more complicated words. When I heard a new one, I always grabbed at it, and even if I had seen a word in writing only once, I usually knew exactly how it was spelt. I enjoyed writing and being good at it. Expressing words in writing was much easier for me than taking the long way round, as I experienced it, via speech.

I used to write labels for various things. I wanted everything to be orderly, clear and separate. This was not some way of keeping an inner chaos under control, but an attempt to arrange the external world according to the same system as my inner world, a way of establishing a slightly better accord between me and everything else. Inside me were already closed compartments with labels attached for events, rooms and worlds. Like a computer, these did indeed have a great many ramifications and sub-departments, but the cross-connections were few. Clearly, the worlds outside me would be easier to relate to if I was able to sort them out in a similar way. So I made labels which said what everything was and where it belonged.

When I had just learnt to write, before I had developed the art of spelling to perfection, I made a label. On it I wrote: GUNILLA. SCRT CASE WICH I HAV THINGS IN AND RNGS ALLSO BRASLETS. My parents thought it was charming that I had made my own jewel-case, and I let them think that. They thought that maybe I was envious of my sister's red jewel-case with a mirror in the lid—my mother had one like it, in white—and they wondered whether *I* wanted one. I certainly did not. I didn't like that kind of thing, but I knew they would never understand. I had my own purpose with this case and its label, but they thought otherwise.

I had—and always had had, as long as I could remember—a great fear of jewellery. That terror also included hairclips and metal buttons. I thought they were frightening, detestable, revolting. If I was made to touch jewellery, I felt a sharp whistling metallic noise in my ears, and my stomach turned over. Like a note falsely electrified, that sound would creep from the base of my spine upwards until it rang in my ears, tumbled down into my throat and settled like nausea in my stomach. These physical sensations produced by jewellery frightened me, and I transferred that terror on to the jewellery itself, so that the very sight of it terrified me.

Some jewellery was worse than others: the smaller and more ornate it was, the more difficult it was to endure. The ornamentation seemed to move and make the jewel or button even more menacing. Objects set with stones were worse than smooth, simple things, and rings were worse than bracelets. Decorative Norwegian sweater buttons were terrible, and I couldn't wear them. I simply couldn't stand them. And brown metal hairclips with horrible little plastic bobbles at the ends were awful, too. They made a sound when you took hold of them—a metal sound that jarred with that smooth, slippery, transparent stuff, the plastic. It was horrible and dangerous, and it hurt inside. And rings with nasty shiny stones in elaborate settings, they also jarred with each other. I hated the slippery shiny sound, and the sharply convoluted setting was painful to me. The convolution didn't stay still so that you could really see what it was. It seemed to be crawling with something. You could hear that in the very word 'convoluted'. Convoluted, convoluted, convoluted. It moved. It was revolting.

But if you said the word very clearly so that all the sounds could be heard—c o n v o l u t e d— then perhaps you could get it to stay still? If you conquered the word completely, perhaps you could influence the actual object, get it to stop, be ordinary and make it into nothing at all? I tried, but no, it didn't work.

I couldn't escape being given trinkets as presents. Rings and bracelets were what a little girl was supposed to like. It gave me the creeps whenever I was given any. Sometimes I managed to escape touching the actual present by opening the box, saying thank you very much, hurrying off to my room to pretend to try it on, then coming out again and saying it looked just right. But on some occasions they insisted on seeing the ring on my finger. I often tried to refuse, but that was difficult. I didn't at all want to put it on. And what did it matter, anyway, whether it was suitable?—I had no intention of wearing it. But I couldn't say that. So the ring would be forced on to my finger, and my heart would be thumping. I stood absolutely still, trying to endure the nausea and the metal fingers that kept pinching my spine. Now the adults were satisfied, and all was well. I had only to thank them for the lovely gift, and then all would be perfect. Perfect. They were very pleased with their own goodness.

So my 'scrt case' came about because at last I had found such a good box for the purpose. A hard plastic one that clicked shut when you pressed down the lid. It was a reliable box to put jewellery into, because nothing could creep out and suddenly appear in some unexpected place. The things would stay preserved inside that box, and I only needed to open it at Christmas or on my birthday to drop into it some new and nauseating present.

When I was arranging the box, I would click the lid up and down time and time again so as to really convince myself that it was secure. That click was a safe sound, meaning properly shut. As I felt I was really helping myself,

I was tremendously pleased when I arranged that box. Then it didn't matter so much that no one else understood. And it felt very good to have succeeded in creating something with two functions: the official one, for them— a little girl's jewellery case; and the other vital and unofficial function, just for me—a place to shut all those disgusting things into. I didn't even have to say anything. They believed 'what it wasn't' all on their own.

My mother had some inkling of my terrors, because she noticed that she couldn't force certain clothing on to me or get me to wear clips in my hair. She probably thought it was simply yet another of my peculiarities. On the other hand, Kerstin knew exactly how frightened I was of certain things, and she occasionally exploited this just to scare me. Perhaps sometimes she simply wanted to get some sort of reaction out of me, and to threaten me with jewellery was a sure way of succeeding. I felt myself more observed than I really was, more understood in an awkward way, when Kerstin took advantage of weaknesses, than I did when my mother, apparently thoughtlessly, didn't even understand which things frightened me. She just thought maybe the cardigan was prickly, or the jersey too small, and that was why I didn't want it. She never realised it was because of the buttons.

All the time I was growing up, I suffered from an almost constant shudder down my spine. Periodically, the shuddering grew worse, while at other times it kept relatively quiet so that I was able to live with it. It was like that feeling the moment before you sneeze, only as if it had got stuck and was suspended inside my spinal cord in order to turn into something permanent. The shudder that wasn't really a shudder *must* be released, then ought to be registered on the Richter scale. I so much wanted it to happen, just as your body wants to sneeze when a sneeze is on the way. But the feeling was there to stay, an eternity of eternities. I became slightly used to it, but it was a constant torture, most noticeable when it changed in intensity. With a wealth of inventiveness, I was able to alleviate it a little at times, but never entirely.

It was like cold steel down my spine. It was hard and fluid at the same time, with metallic fingers lightly drumming and tickling on the outside. Like sharp clips digging into my spine, and lemonade inside. Icy heat and digging fiery cold. It was like the sound of screeching chalk against a blackboard turned into a silent concentration of feeling, then placed at the back of my neck. Placed at the nape of my neck for ever. From there, so metallic, the feeling rang in my ears, radiated out into my arms, clipped itself firmly into my elbows, but never came to an end. Never ever came to an end.

I never told anyone it felt like that. I didn't know it could be any other way, and I had no words with which to describe my torment. Such words didn't exist. I had become used to it, but when it got worse, when the pressure increased, I had to do something to quieten it. Rubbing my hands together could help, and pressing my back and the nape of my neck hard against a wall could also relieve it. Sometimes it helped a little to jerk my head. I had to feel my way ahead and try to find ways that might alleviate it.

I began to develop compulsive rituals. By running the tips of my fingers or pressing the palm of my hand against something, the shuddering might first increase but then reach a point where I no longer felt it so acutely. As if I could raise its frequency so that it lay beyond what I could perceive.

Curved things were what I wanted to touch. I grasped every door-handle I passed. I put the tip of my forefinger just where the handle curved. This felt good. I followed the banister rail with my hand all the way to the middle where it curved, then stopped and rubbed my palm back and forth on the curve. I did that every time I went up or down the stairs, and always at the same spot. I had to do it every time to calm my spine. I always finished off my walk down the stairs by scraping my nails against the rounded bit at the end of the rail. I had great feeling in my nails, just like in my teeth, and in some strange way I even had some feeling in my hair.

To quieten my spine, I would feel with my fingertips under every bottle I saw, in the curved hollow base. It had to be all the bottles—I was not to miss any of them. If I didn't feel under every single one, the whole exercise was flawed, and I did so want it to be perfect and complete and finished. I wanted the shuddering to come to an end at some point. At last quieten and come to an end. And it did to some extent—anyway, the worst of it. Just that, interrupting the eternity, was my fixation. I couldn't bear that shuddering in me devouring my energy and taking all my attention, but I didn't know how to get rid of it. From the point of view of my feelings, rubbing the palm of my hand and scraping with my nails were fairly logical and creative ways of trying to overcome my torment. But this was disturbing, foolish, irritating and incomprehensible to everyone else. They had no other alternative to offer than that I should pull myself together and stop all this nonsense. They had no plaster, whether pretend or genuine, to put on my spine. They never expressed any compassion. They didn't even see that I was tormented.

My father even thought my suffering was amusing. It was a performance put on to entertain him, and he used my upbringing as an excuse to amuse himself at my expense. He thought he had to stop me carrying out the rituals that were so important to me. Naturally, he could do that, for however obstinate I was, it was inescapable that he was almost two metres tall and much stronger than I was. He held the bottles at arm's length and laughed at my anguish when I tried to reach them. My stupid, nonsensical tricks gave him and his world the right to make a fool of me.

A few bottles couldn't possibly be so important, could they?

I pummelled him. I reached out. I needed to touch under that bottle with my fingers. I had to. I pushed and lunged and whined. If I managed to get quite close, he moved the bottle further away. My urgent need meant that I often won in the end, and when he had finished amusing himself, I was finally given the bottle. While they all laughed, I was at last allowed to touch underneath. But it hurt. I was wretched because of their laughter, and their behaviour created little desire in me to be any closer to them. All the same, though, I was relieved to be allowed to do what was necessary. For him this was nothing, just stupid tricks that he forgot soon after they had occurred. A child's silly ideas which had entertained him for a moment.

'There's nothing to sulk about. Haha.'

To me it was as painful as if by his laughter he had stopped me eating, sleeping or going to the lavatory when I needed to. Perhaps even worse.

I had another *idée fixe* at this age, which lasted for a while—that I should not sit where anyone else had recently sat. If anyone got up out of an armchair or other chair, I couldn't sit on it.

'I can't sit on your seat,' I would tell them. They ought not to sit just anyhow on a chair, I thought, as they ruined it for me. I thought it stupid that they sat on different chairs just for a short while. Couldn't they plan their sitting better, so that I could have a chair in peace and quiet? I wanted to teach them about sitting on chairs, but they laughed at me and said I couldn't make decisions for them. I actually thought it smelt peculiar for a long time after someone had got up off a chair, and I didn't want to sit down until the smell had gone. But there was no point in telling them that, because they would just go over and sniff and say with absolute certainty that it didn't smell of anything. So I preferred to stand up.

This period when I sometimes stood at the dining-table because someone had recently sat on my chair didn't last all that long, perhaps six months. Then I no longer smelt any particular smells from chairs, and never thought about whether anyone had sat there before me.

Our family spent most holidays in Åland, but the summer when I was five we took a different cottage from usual. My mother had had her own way over the change, for like me, my father didn't like going to new places. This cottage was larger than the one we had rented the year before, and there were lots of terrifying cows outside. I didn't like this new place and I was scared of the cows. I wanted to be where we'd been before. It was a hot summer, and Kerstin was devoured by mosquitoes, while I, as usual, didn't get a single bite. The sun blazed down, my sister was all swollen, my parents were quarrelling and I didn't want to go out of the house because of the cows.

One day my father found a windmill quite near the cottage, and we were to go and look at it, Kerstin, father and me. We climbed up a ladder on to a platform, a narrow balcony all round the mill, where there was a door. Kerstin tried it and it turned out to be unlocked, so she opened it, cautiously—after all, this was someone's house. When she saw it was furnished like a little doll's house, she couldn't resist it and went inside. Pappa saw this as a chance to frighten the life out of her in his 'joky' way. He closed the door and hooked over the hasp. I didn't grasp what he was doing. He signalled irritably to me to get down the ladder and called out ' 'Bye then, we're off now!' through the door to Kerstin. Then, exalted by his 'joke' but irritated that I hadn't realised I was to get down, he turned to me again and beckoned brusquely—he was in a hurry now. We had to make our way down quickly, so that Kerstin would be left alone and afraid, shut inside a strange house. But I couldn't get down the ladder by myself. I had no sense of where my arms and legs were, so how would I be able to get down a ladder? But I sensed his annoyance and that I had to get a move on. I fumbled for the rung of the ladder with my foot, but fell. As I fell, I saw stills from my life passing in front of my eyes. My five-year-old life flickered past me like a comic strip, and for a moment I knew I was going to die.

I didn't die. After tumbling over in the air, I landed on my head on the stony ground below. Everything went black and empty, and nothing in my head. Then I saw mother running towards us, and Kerstin, now released from the windmill, was talking about juice and a plaster. Then I lost consciousness again. When I woke up, I was in the car with a rug round me. That was strange, because we never used that rug. It was always kept in the boot with a whole lot of other things on top of it. But now it was round me and I didn't know how it had got there.

After a while we came to a house called a hospital, and there I had to sit on a stool in front of a doctor who tapped me on my knee. I knew you should kick up your leg when you were tapped on the knee. I'd seen that in Donald Duck, so I did so. I always tried to think out, to calculate, what I should do in order to do the right thing.

After the visit to the hospital we went back to the cottage. I had concussion and was to take it easy, to be still and rest a lot. But my parents didn't think they could stay at home with me all the time, because that would be hard on Kerstin. They went off swimming sometimes, all of them, leaving me at home. I had wanted to go swimming too. I loved the water—I didn't feel anything like as clumsy in it as I did on land. But I had to stay at home and lie still, even though I didn't feel ill. Before they left they would pull down the blinds in the bedroom, although it was the middle of the day, and tell me I had to rest. I had no desire to rest, so each time they left I got up and jumped up and down on the bed.

'That's why you are what you are,' Kerstin often used to say to me, half-joking, when we were older. She meant my fall from the windmill, and I used to think that it was perhaps because I jumped on the bed when I should have lain still. Kerstin said it half-jokingly, but we both knew that I simply was as I was, that I was different in some special way, although everyone else pretended it wasn't so. But we didn't know why.

Had I not ruined my father's joke at the windmill with my accident, what would have happened, no doubt, is that we would have walked a little way away and then, when enough time had elapsed for Kerstin to think we really had gone, and that it was no joke, he would have gone back and let her out. He was totally incapable of putting himself in another person's place. Just as when he wanted to prove that cats always landed on all fours, regardless of how they fell. No one had questioned his statement, but he wanted to prove it all the same, because it was such fun being right. So he caught Knatte, our cat, in the garden and, ignoring all protests, he carried him up to my room, which had the highest window in the house, a long way from the ground. He opened the window, turned Knatte upside down, and hung him by his paws. He swung the cat a little, then flung him, paws uppermost, out through the window.

'Now look,' he said. 'Watch carefully, and you'll see that a cat always lands on its paws.'

But I didn't want to look. And Knatte who, to Pappa's delight, of course turned in the air and landed on his paws, hurt himself and limped for a long time afterwards. My father thought that kind of thing fun.

Five

The day had arrived when it was no longer possible to keep the world at bay, the day that led to a state of shock that lasted for ten years. The day when playschool was to begin. They had told me it would be fun to go to playschool, and I had believed them. I thought that meant they knew it would be fun. They said so.

'It'll be fun and you'll make friends.'

I thought that meant they really did know about the future, although for the life of me I couldn't fathom how they could know anything that had not yet happened. I quite literally took their word for it. I had no real idea what or who those 'friends' were, but I thought that perhaps I was to go to a party and have cream-cake. However, that was not the way it was to be.

My mother took me there the first day. I didn't know what playschool entailed. I had no picture of what it might be like. When we went into the hall, the noise, the movement and all the children showered down on me and overwhelmed my senses within half a second. I had never seen so many children before, and I was terrified. I stiffened and refused to move. No. I won't. Not in all these rooms and with all these children. No. They had said fun, but everything looked terrible. And felt terrible.

We stood in the hall with the helper. The other children had gone on in. My mother was about to leave. I suddenly realised she was going, and it was too much for me. Sheer panic took over.

No! Where was I? Where had all these empty faces come from? What did they want of me? I didn't want to be here.

Leave me alone! I couldn't feel where I began or ended. Was I going live here now? Was this awful place to be my new home?

No! I must get away from here. I must get out. Let me out! Let me go! I must get away from all this noise and all these empty faces.

I couldn't stay, I just couldn't. I kicked and screamed. I bit and scratched and clawed. Embarrassed, my mother took me back home. I did everything I could to avoid going back again, to that horrible place called playschool. I had never seen so many empty faces, and in such confusion, before. I hadn't known that there were so many, or that they could be so empty. I felt nothing but profound terror.

Everyone I didn't know had an empty face, which meant everyone except my family. I didn't realise that these faces were people in the same way as those I knew were people. Those faces were as lacking in content as furniture, and I thought that, just like furniture, they belonged in the rooms I saw them in. I didn't consider them as either children or adults, able to move between different rooms of their own volition—any more than a sofa could. *I* could go from room to room, I knew that. But if I first saw someone I didn't know in one room, and then saw him or her in another, I thought it wasn't the same person. To me the face was empty, and there was nothing in it to tell me that I had met him or her before.

It confused me totally when someone said that he or she had seen something I had been doing in a different room—*I* had to know someone really well for a face to have any significance. Not in my wildest fantasies could I imagine that that person had actually been there, in that room, then. It seemed as crazy as if someone had said that the same furniture was in all the rooms I was in, that the chairs and tables followed me wherever I went. I pondered on these strange situations and occasionally

tried to test things out by doing something forbidden, and then seeing who knew about it. This seldom threw any light on the matter, but it did contribute something to a parallel theory of mine, that those people I did know—the ones with meaningful faces—could perhaps see into all the rooms, always. It would have been the logical counterweight to the empty faces not being able to move at all from room to room. I tried to understand, but had no tools with which to do so, although I did have the intellectual capacity. My grasp of time was of something that grew more rapidly in breadth than in length, so to speak—from then, to now, and on into the future. My view of time and my view of space belonged together—time was a one-storey doll's house which grew irregularly, with new rooms in various directions.

Time and again I was very hurt when people said they knew things about me, things which, according to my view of how it was, they couldn't know. The only tactic I had for dealing with this was to ignore it completely. I thought that best, but what I didn't know then was that nothing in *their* world makes people so furious as being ignored. To me, being ignored by others was pleasant, and didn't disturb me in the slightest. So I didn't at all understand the agitation of grown-ups when I took no notice of them. They really were a mystery to me. Sometimes I might ignore other people simply because everything was so unfathomable, but that was much more subconscious. Then I would just turn in on myself and switch off, so that major incomprehensibles could no longer clutter up my mind.

There was something special about the way I saw things. My vision was rather flat, two-dimensional in a way, and this was somehow important to the way I viewed space and people. I seemed to have to fetch visual impressions from my eyes. Visual impressions did not come to *me.* Nor did my vision provide me with any automatic priority in what I saw—everything seemed to appear just as clearly and with the same sharpness of image. The world looked like a photograph, and this had a variety of consequences. I didn't realise that the houses I saw along our street had anything inside them. I saw everything as if it was scenery. Although I knew that our house had space inside it, I never connected that bit of knowledge with the house opposite. That one was as flat as a sheet of paper. The people, the empty faces that I sometimes saw in the gardens outside the houses, I saw as some kind of stage props belonging to the scenery. I didn't think there could be people actually living inside, in the same way as my family lived in our house.

Another consequence of my way of seeing the world was this. It was quite clear to me that a certain object could be behind or under another object. If I saw that, I understood it, but connected it only with what I saw. The moment I saw a ball rolling under a bureau, I knew that balls could be found under bureaux. I also realised the ball was there even when I couldn't see it, and I was able to generalise sufficiently to realise that other balls might be concealed by large pieces of furniture. Furthermore, I was able to add these experiences to my knowledge of the world and apply them in the future. But they gave me no inkling that there might be other things besides balls under the bureau, or, indeed, that anything at all might end up under or behind other things so as to be no longer visible.

My parents mocked and scolded me for my hopeless laziness. The way it looked from their world was as if I couldn't even be bothered to lift anything up to search for whatever I was looking for. Had God ever created a lazier child? Haha.

I could not refuse indefinitely to go to playschool. After refusing for a week, I was quite simply made to go back. This time they tried to prepare a slightly calmer reception for me. My mother and I were met in the hall. The other children had already arrived and were busy in other rooms. I was shown a hook on the wall and told that it was mine, and my jacket was hung on it. Mamma had said we were only there on a visit and we weren't going to stay. She'd promised me that. Now we'd been there and hung my jacket on the hook, I wanted to go home. Couldn't we go home now?

I had seen a woodwork bench in the hall and a boy sawing something at it. He was making a jigsaw puzzle, and it had looked really rather exciting. I agreed to go back the next day if I was allowed to make a puzzle. They would be sure to allow me to do that, mother said. I had worked out that then I wouldn't have go into those other rooms where the children were, but could stay in the hall.

The second day we went, I hadn't realised that this time my mother was going to leave me there. But she pushed me into the hall, and hurried away. I didn't know whether or when she was coming back. I was now alone in this awful place, but I tried my best to stick it out. Everything was nasty and strange and new and different and muddled, and I had to be just as usual. I had to be more than just as usual. I had to play at playschool and be any ordinary child. I had not to be me.

I said to the empty face, to Miss, that I wanted to make a puzzle. I was told that was really for boys, but she would make an exception for me. She fetched a piece of wood, a pencil and a rubber. I sat on my own at a table. The other children were somewhere else.

She explained what I was to do: 'Like this and like this and like this. Likethisandlikethisandlikethisandlikethis-andlikethis . . .'

Then she went away. I had no idea what she had said. It had all gone much too fast, but it didn't worry me that I hadn't understood. I knew what a puzzle was.

I often did puzzles at home. My father had a puzzle

with several thousand pieces, and he used to ask me to help. My sharp eyes meant that I would find the right bit of puzzle among the thousands of others. Father used to show me the place where the bit should go, and I would find it. Mostly, I was allowed to help for only a little while, because I spoilt the pleasure for him when it was so easy for me. I would have liked to help more. I was proud of being good at something, proud of being able to help, and I couldn't understand why he didn't want any more help from me. I thought that was the point, that fitting all the bits into their right places was the point of the puzzle. If that was the case, he ought to accept all the help he could get so that it was finished as quickly as possible—so that he could start another puzzle from the beginning and finish it, then begin on another.

I had puzzles of my own, too, with five hundred and a thousand pieces, but it was not such fun doing them by myself. It was much more fun being better than father at *his* puzzle. I really thought about puzzles more as phenomena than as things actually to do. A puzzle was something that had a beginning and an end, and I liked things that were finished. A finished, completed thing was satisfying. So I wanted to do a puzzle only once, and then that was that. The thought of emptying out the bits and starting all over again from the beginning seemed quite absurd. If it was finished it was finished.

That was my experience of puzzles as I sat at the table in playschool with a pencil and piece of wood. I didn't see how there could be a thousand pieces from that little piece of wood, but I realised I must draw a complicated picture—otherwise, the puzzle would be much too easy to do. I thought the point must be that I should draw something really good on the wood, that I should draw the actual picture the puzzle was supposed to reproduce. I knew I was good at drawing, but I made an extra-special effort all the same. I wanted Miss to think it was really good. I wanted her to say that what I had done was good.

'That's wrong,' she said when I showed her. 'You can't saw that out.'

I realised it was wrong, but not how it was wrong. I had no inner picture of what to saw something meant, or how it occurred. Miss turned my piece of wood over and told me to start again.

I drew another picture on the back—a really fine and interesting picture. But that was wrong, too. Now Miss was cross and said that I hadn't listened to her. I didn't realise that she had meant, presumably, that I should draw the contours of the puzzle pieces. With my inner image of a thousand bits, it would have seemed very peculiar to ask such a thing of a child. All I understood was that whenever I tried to do my very best, it was wrong.

Later, I tried to find a way of understanding why it had been wrong. I asked at home how puzzles were made and was told that the bits were pressed out by big machines. So didn't people cut out the bits? No, they didn't—puzzles were made in factories. I was none the wiser about what Miss had wanted me to do. It ended up in my inner pigeon-hole for absolute incomprehensibles. In that compartment, questions seemed to stay as if preserved, perhaps for several years, and when I had an opportunity to take them out again they were quite fresh. I often did that, trying to understand things by asking questions long after the actual event with which they were connected. People didn't understand what I was aiming at and thought I was just asking something, anything, that occurred to me. But my questions were mostly asked in order to understand properly something I had thought a lot about. Sometimes I might suddenly associate an inner colour in a situation with an event that was there among the old incomprehensibles and that had the same colour. Then I would try to make the most of the occasion and ask questions in order to understand the unfathomable.

Nothing came of the puzzle at playschool. Miss took the piece of wood away, and instead gave me a plastic board with pegs on it. I was to fit plastic beads on to them. She said it would perhaps be best if I did something the other girls did. I went back to playschool the next day, and then again the day after that. At first I didn't understand that just because I was fetched one day, I would also be fetched the next day.

In the end I grasped that I really would be fetched and that I wasn't going to live there. But I wasn't really clear about *when* my mother would come. I had no inner sense that I was there for roughly the same period of time every day. Everything seemed to be simply a matter of chance. My mother just appeared and we were to go home. It never even occurred to me that the other children also went home when I did, even though I saw them putting on their jackets and shoes when I did. I didn't know that the other adults I saw might be their parents come to collect them. I believed the children belonged to the playschool. I thought they lived there—or anyway, that they could only exist there.

I very much wanted to understand, and that led me to think up something, a theory about how things worked, that always applied to whatever I saw. Every time my mother came, one thing was always the same: she always came into the hall. What if that meant I had to be in the hall for her to come at all? That's what it was. That must be it, I thought. If she came and I wasn't in the hall, if she didn't see me, would she then go home again? And perhaps it also meant that if I wanted to go home, then she would appear if I went out into the hall. I had actually never seen my mother in any other room except the hall, so I associated her appearance with the actual room, as if she just materialised in the doorway. Everything had to hang together in some logical way and now I had probably found it: as long as I was in the hall, the room to which mother always came, then she would come. If on the other hand I was in the wrong room, in any of the rooms into which she never came, then she wouldn't come.

Every moment when I wasn't being watched, I slipped out into the hall and sat on the floor there. It was a better place to be, a calmer place, where I could sit and hope to be fetched sooner.

Irritably, they would fetch me out of the hall and say I was to stay with the other children. I couldn't think why I wasn't allowed to be left in peace. The noise the children made was torment to me, and I couldn't shut it out. I heard what everyone said and saw what everyone was doing. It frightened me and wore me out. One of the grown-ups occasionally let me take a table and chair out into the hall so that I could sit there in peace putting plastic beads on to the bead-board. She realised I wanted to be left on my own and I sat there making patterns with colours. I could make quite complicated patterns. I was proud when lots of people thought my bead patterns were outstandingly good, but at the same time it was rather boring making them. Although I liked sorting beads into colours and patterns, I would have liked to do something else. Two terms were rather a long time to spend threading plastic beads on to white pegs. But the bead-boards were the only things on offer for a girl who was unable to play.

The bead-boards were instead of something else, and I sensed that. And I was paying the price of dullness to be allowed to sit alone in the hall. Solitariness and silence hung soft in the air around me. I also had to pay another price to be allowed to sit there—the price of gratitude. Just as later on at school, if I was ever granted special treatment and allowed to do something on my own, then I was sure to be made aware of the fact that it was a favour and that I should be grateful.

Well, just this once then . . . but you mustn't think . . .

We must be fair and consider the other children ... it mustn't become a habit.

The few times I escaped this kind of response, when someone just allowed me a favour without any special admonitions, I could almost feel the disapproval of other adults over how pampered I was.

When I went to playschool in the mornings, I would hang my jacket up on a hook in the hall, any old hook. I had never heard of hanging clothes on special hooks before. We didn't do that at home, or anywhere else I'd been. That picture of a snail couldn't have anything to do with me, could it? There were pictures like that by every hook. When I'd hung my jacket up, some child or other would always sooner or later cry out: 'Miss! She's taken my hook again.'

But I protested, because I knew perfectly well that I hadn't *taken* anything. Taking things was stealing, and I knew I hadn't done that. They said I was stupid to deny something that was so obvious. I felt completely bewildered.

I knew I hadn't taken anything and I couldn't think how a hook on the wall could be mine. That was far too abstract. To me, *my* hook would be a hook I could put in my pocket. How could that hook fastened to the wall be mine? In that case did it mean that no one else could use it, even if I wasn't there? I thought a lot about it. When I gradually accepted that that snail did have something to do with me and that for some unfathomable reason it was important that I hung my jacket just there, I had another problem—finding the snail.

Things that were very similar in colour, shape and size, despite my sharp vision, could merge together and I found it difficult to distinguish one from another. Maybe this was because the creatures portrayed in the pictures had no real content for me. I saw this one was a snail and I also knew what a snail was, but a picture of a snail created no associations in me. So I looked at the shapes in the pictures—all alike; then the size—all alike; then the colours—also alike. And so, even though I wanted to do it correctly, I went on hanging my jacket on the wrong hook.

I couldn't work out the point of the other children. What were they for? I could see that they seemed to know each other, but I didn't understand how that came about. Perhaps that was why I was the only one who didn't live there? The others knew I was different. Children seem to sniff that out long before adults do. They thought I was strange, and I was quickly associated with another strange child in the group, Peter, a fat boy who wore glasses and nappies.

'Peter and Gunilla,' they said, as if we had something to do with each other.

But surely I had nothing in common with him? I was just as uninterested in him as in anyone else. And I didn't wear nappies. I couldn't understand the connection the others made between him and me. Also, he played with the girls in the dolls' corner when he was not allowed to be with the boys. I didn't play with anyone.

One day when I was walking past the dolls' corner where some children were playing, one of them turned to me and said sternly, 'You can't come in here.'

I took that to mean that I could never go in there, never ever. I took it exactly as she said it—you can't come in here. That didn't make me particularly miserable. I had had no intention of going in there anyway, but I didn't really understand why I wasn't *allowed* to. However, as I wasn't allowed to, I never went into the dolls' corner again. Not until the end of term when a photographer came to playschool. The idea was that he should photograph the girls a few at a time in the dolls' corner, but I refused.

'No!'

I knew I wasn't allowed in there. I knew it was forbidden, even if I didn't know why.

The grown-ups and the photographer tried pushing me into the dolls' corner. The table was laid with plastic cups and plates, and they kept talking and shoving me in towards the corner. Finally, I allowed myself to be persuaded. But I never understood why I had to be photographed in there with a doll on my knee, when I never played there.

I got to know the name of one of the children in my playschool group. This was Pia, who really enjoyed being nasty to me. All the attention she paid me meant that her face ceased to be empty, acquired some content and was filled with the name of Pia. I was easy prey for Pia's malevolence because I was so easily deceived. But as a victim, I was regarded as rather unpredictable. I didn't always grasp the malevolence, and I didn't always react as expected.

Pia found out that what really terrified me was to be shut inside the school store-room. The light-switch for the store-room was on the outside, so when she shut me in, she switched the light out too. There I was in the pitch-dark with no night vision, so my eyes couldn't gradually get used to the dark or distinguish a little more. They seemed to have been taken away from me, and I lost all sense of where I was inside that room. I lost my body. The up and downness of things vanished. I couldn't feel what was me and what was the room. It was somehow as if I had totally changed substance, perhaps been turned into gas. A kind of dissolving.

Pia lured me into the store-room over and over again. I couldn't connect the one event with the other and calculate what would happen, particularly as she would find various excuses for us to go there each day. Look at this. Look at that. I'll give you something. Would you like some chewing gum? Shall we go and get some paper? Come on!

Then suddenly, without my really knowing how it happened, she was outside and I was alone in the dark, totally petrified in there. I couldn't move or even feel the door. I didn't know in which direction the door should be, inside there in the pitch-dark. I didn't know where my self was. I felt nothing but stark terror.

Sometimes they found me in there. My terror was an inner state that they couldn't see on me.

'What are you doing in here? Go out to the other children.'

Pia also used the store-room as a threat. If you don't do this I'll shut you in the store-room. If you don't go and get that, I'll shut you in the store-room.

I would never have considered turning to any of the assistants for help. I knew you couldn't do that. But they occasionally heard her and realised what had happened. Then they tried to talk to me. 'You don't have to go to the store-room with her,' they would say.

That didn't have much effect. I didn't understand. What did they mean, didn't have to?

'Tell her that if she tries being silly to you, you'll go and fetch us. Just say, if you're silly then I'll go and fetch someone. Just say that,' they said. I had to repeat it several times, but in the end I grasped what they wanted me to say. I had learnt what I should say.

Soon enough, the two of us stood facing each other once again in the middle of the store-room, Pia nearest to the door, on her way out in order to shut me inside.

'If you're silly, I'll go and fetch someone,' I said.

'Yes, you do that,' said Pia.

And nothing happened except that she did what she usually did. She went out, closed the door and switched off the light. I couldn't understand anything. I had thought that those words I was to say would stop her from shutting me in. That it was a sort of chant that would somehow stop her. I hadn't realised that I had to *do* something as well. I had only learnt to repeat it like an incantation. The words meant nothing.

Six

There were climbing-frames in the playground, one of them red and blue and shaped like an igloo with a hole in the top. I liked it very much, and always wanted to climb on it. But that was impossible, because the presence of all the other children created such turmoil that I couldn't concentrate on climbing. I couldn't take the risk of climbing up something, then half-way up suddenly losing all sense of direction and balance. Carrying out anything to do with movement required my total presence of mind, my total control. Adults, of course, couldn't make out why one day I could climb up something, alone, and another day, with others there, I couldn't climb at all. They couldn't see the difference. It could only be due to reluctance, defiance, laziness or at best shyness. Somehow *I* knew the difference between when I could and when I couldn't, but inside me there were few words with which to explain it. And the words I did have were hard to get out.

Out in the playground I mostly stood about on my own, and although I was often cold and wanted to go indoors, it was a relief to be outside. The confusion that twenty children managed to achieve was less tangible here. My greatest desire was to be alone indoors when the others were outside, but that was inconceivable. Why should I be allowed to go in when no one else was? That would be unfair, and the others might be envious.

Envious. I didn't really know what that was, nor could I imagine it. I had never thought, abstractly, that I should like to be in someone else's place. When I wished for things, my wishes were quite independent of anything others had or hadn't got. They told me that Pia was envious, and that was why she spoilt my things. She would go into the store-room and tip all the beads off my beadboards, or else she wrote her name on them and said that she had made them.

My mother thought that my problems at playschool, now that I had at last agreed it was necessary to go there, were to do with being bored. The year before, she had already thought that I was intellectually mature enough to go to proper school, and perhaps this was partly true. I could already read and write, and much of what playschool had to offer—play—I thought seemed childish.

'Who did you play with today?' she would ask in an anxious, rather uncertain voice on our way home. I could hear that she wanted me to have played with someone. I wanted to answer because I wanted to oblige, and I also wanted to answer so as to be left in peace afterwards, not to be asked any more.

'Pia,' I would reply.

This was a logical answer. Pia was one of the few children whose names I knew, and she also paid a great deal of attention to me. The difference between bullying and play was not all that obvious to me. My mother was either relieved or pleased that I had been playing with someone, and she thought she would help me acquire a real friend. So she contacted Pia's parents, and it was decided that I should spend an evening a week at their place while my mother was at her evening class.

I knew nothing about what had been decided. Perhaps Mamma mentioned it to me, but I could form no inner picture of going to Pia's house, so even if I did hear her, what she said didn't stick in my mind. Pia was connected with playschool and I couldn't possibly have imagined that she might have parents and a home that I could go to.

It was a tremendous shock when suddenly one evening I was left there. The terror and uncertainty I always felt when faced with new environments now left me entirely at the mercy of Pia. And she noticed.

Pia's family also had a dog that frightened me. Dogs were much more unpredictable than cats when it came to sounds and quick movements, and, never having known a dog, I'd never got used to them. I was scared of them, and when we were out I always used to try to get my mother to cross over if a dog was coming along the pavement. A sudden bark, or a dog jumping up at me, made my sensory faculties distort my perception, so that the dog became the size of an elephant and everything solid around me seemed to dissolve and sway and float.

Pia quickly discovered that by shutting me in their garage together with the dog, then switching the light off from outside, she could utterly terrify me. But I didn't scream, and never told on her. In some peculiar way, I thought that this was sure to be right—it *should* be like this—since here, too, there was a light that could be switched off from the outside. Apart from playschool, I had never been anywhere else where lights of this kind existed, so I really did believe that the lighting arrangement somehow justified her shutting me in.

Perhaps my silence also made her go on—the fact that my reaction was so minimal although my terror was so great. I became silent, was totally paralysed. If I didn't stay completely, absolutely still, then I would explode with terror. I could hear the dog moving about in the dark.

I was let out in the end, but I never knew how long I had been shut in. Inside, there was no time. Pia said it was good for me to be hardened. She was helping me, she said, and what happened in the garage would toughen me up. She now had a perfect weapon with which to threaten me. 'If you don't . . . I'll shut you in the garage.'

I would do absolutely anything rather than be with that

dog in the dark garage. I, who could protest so violently, who could obstinately refuse to do things at home, never even thought to do that here. I felt completely abandoned, I had no choice.

'Go up to Mum and Dad and ask if they've been fucking,' Pia said firmly.

'What?' I said.

'Go upstairs and say this: "Have you two been fucking?"'

'What does that mean?'

'I can't explain what it means, but they'll be pleased, I promise. Go on, do it now. If you don't, I'll shut you in the garage.'

I went upstairs and asked the question. Three faces— the mother's, the father's and the older sister's—turned towards me with expressions of obvious disgust. Now they also knew what a badly brought up, insolent, horrible child I was.

At this time, I also had a vague theory that perhaps my mother, and other people I was familiar with, knew about everything that happened to me, even if they weren't present. There seemed to be a great deal to indicate that they knew things that I couldn't understand *how* they could know.

'That's enough now . . . You don't need that . . . You're tired . . . You can't be hungry now.'

Nor had I any idea that grown-ups could talk about me when I wasn't present and in that way find out things. Also, they often seemed to know about the future.

'It'll be all right . . . You'll be asked to parties once you're older . . . It won't hurt . . . You'll enjoy it.'

I thought my theory was quite logical. The vacant faces in my world, all those I didn't know well, had nothing to do with me and so couldn't know anything at all about me. They couldn't move from one place to another. So a counterbalance to the existence of these empty faces

79

with their non-movement and non-knowing might well be that the people I did actually know, the ones who had recognisable faces, could be everywhere without my being able to see them—and therefore they knew everything. When it came to Pia, the theory became painful, for what if my mother knew how nasty Pia was to me? Why, then, did she leave me there, week after week, for me to be tormented? There must be a reason. I tried to think out what the connection was, but I couldn't fathom it.

At home, I played with my sister when I wasn't occupied on my own, or simply behind or under some piece of furniture. I could play only with Kerstin, of course, who knew precisely my way of playing; she would steer the games, decide for me, and invent everything. But she had grown older, and had started to have more friends of her own. I didn't like this. It made the difference between us much clearer, and meant that I felt I couldn't play with other children. I wanted Kerstin to be with me, instead, when her friends came to our house. When I tried to be with them, I usually failed by not understanding what they were doing. So I disturbed them all the time. I would go into Kerstin's room and be assertive. I didn't sense that she wanted to be left alone with her friends. I just wanted them to go home.

Otherwise, I was mostly helpful, although hardly anyone noticed. I really did want to be obliging—once I was able to understand what that entailed—but many times I didn't, and then it all went wrong.

Lazy. Doesn't listen. Doesn't help. Careless. Inattentive. Drags her feet. Hears only what she wants to hear. Sulks.

In the end I could no longer find the energy to want to help. There seemed no point. So I just gave way to their image of me, and helpfulness was replaced by suspicion. And as I had no real respect for adults—I didn't think they had anything to do with me—I sometimes displayed an insolence that took their breath away. They

80

couldn't reach me. Somehow, because they weren't important to me, I became inviolable to them.

My behaviour could really shock adults. They simply couldn't believe a six-year-old could be so difficult to get through to. I was an entire resistance movement in one small body. One day when one of Kerstin's friends came to see us with her mother and younger sister, it was decided that the mothers would have coffee together and that I should be with the three-year-old. I was to take her up to my room and play with her. We were to have fruit juice and biscuits there in my room, and my mother had laid a tray for us. I didn't understand—I was never allowed to eat anything in my room when I wanted to, so why should I suddenly do so now? It was awfully strange to have fruit juice and biscuits in my room, and I had no intention of touching it—something was wrong. I didn't think the little sister should have any, either. We weren't *allowed* to eat in our rooms. That was an old rule, and mother couldn't very well change it by suddenly putting a tray in there.

We stood in my room, the three-year-old and I, and I didn't know what to do with her. She was just an empty face, a younger sister, a little kid looking at me in a silly way that I couldn't interpret. I wasn't usually violent with other children, but something made me hit her with a clothes hanger. Perhaps I wanted to see whether she was like me and would put up with it in silence, whether there was some common denominator between us because we were both younger sisters. Perhaps I wanted to find out what an empty face really was and what happened when you hit it. I banged her on the head with the hanger, hard, but she wasn't the same sort of younger sister as I was. She wasn't quiet when I hit her. Instead she ran bawling out of my room and down the stairs to her mother.

I could hear angry voices coming from down below.

81

Then I heard her indignant mother coming up the stairs to tell me off. She thought she would scold me because I had hit her daughter, but she didn't know it was a guerrilla warfare zone she was now trying to invade. And I was inventive when it came to protecting myself.

No, she was not to come in. I had decided that, and I decided things for myself. That mother had nothing to do with me. I would die if she came anywhere near me. She must go away.

Indignant people always frightened me. They moved so oddly, jerking their heads, their hands shaking and their voices so peculiar. Lightning could leap out of their mouths—psst!—it came so quickly you couldn't make it out. With people I knew, I had some chance of calculating how they would behave, but others were totally unpredictable in these situations. And as I couldn't bear unpredictability, it was particularly threatening when they hovered there outside in their world, without even considering whether they had any right to step into mine. So it was urgent to stop that woman from coming anywhere near me.

I fetched the jug of fruit juice from my room. I took it with me out on to the landing, which jutted out from the curved staircase. And when the mother was just below me, I turned the jug upside down and emptied it all over her. Her yellow hair went absolutely flat and transparent on top, and I was terribly surprised to be able to see right through it. The red juice ran all over her clothes. She looked up with her mouth wide open, but said nothing. She looked funny.

The juice worked just as I had hoped. That mother did not continue on up the stairs. A moment later, when I looked out through the upper balcony door, I saw her going out through the gate with her children. She had a scarf round her head so I couldn't see it any longer, which was a pity—I would have liked to have another look at her transparent hair. She was hurrying down the gravel path, holding a child by each hand. The children seemed to be hanging behind her, finding it difficult to keep up. My mother and Kerstin were now angry with me, but I could endure that. Their habitual anger was nothing compared to the anger of a stranger.

At the end of my last term at playschool, the time had come to take the test for proper school. I had been ill when the test had been held at my projected school, so I was now going to go to another one. My mother and I went by bus. I didn't know where we were going, but I did notice that it was an unusual day. Going by bus was tremendously unusual. When we arrived, we walked across a square and then in through an entrance to an unfamiliar square white building. This was a modern suburb with buildings like boxes, and I had never seen anything like it before. We might just as well have been on the moon. A lady—an empty face—met us in the hall of this alien building.

When mother was about to leave, I was terrified. Was she just going to abandon me here? The fact that I had learnt that I was fetched every day from playschool was not something I could transfer to this situation. It didn't help me to work out that I would probably be fetched from this strange place too. What had happened at playschool had no relevance here. Everything to do with playschool was in a special compartment in my mind which could only be opened when I was there, at playschool.

I tried refusing to stay, but my mother simply went and so I had to stay. I was led into a room where, to my horror, there was a man and a lot of children. The man and the lady . . . A man and a woman. Were they my new mother and father? Was I to live here now? But all these children? Help! I didn't want to be here. At first, my reluctance to stay became a paralysing terror, but after a bit I resigned myself to adapting to the situation. Yet again the world had been jerked from under my feet. All the others seemed to be ordinary and normal . . . I just had to try to put up with whatever those vacant faces wanted of me.

What they wanted, for some reason, was that I should put some building blocks together according to a pattern on a piece of paper that they gave me. Then, they put a sentence in front of me and asked me to say what the letters in it were. But I could already read. So I read the sentence instead. They asked me again what the letters were called, so I read the whole sentence again. Why should I say what the letters were when I could read the words? It seemed silly. *I* knew that I knew what they were called.

I always did that when I didn't understand why people asked me something: I answered with what I thought, and repeated it over and over again. I didn't understand that when they repeated their question, they meant they wanted another answer. The man and the lady looked troubled, but said I was a clever girl.

I tried to work out whether those blocks they'd wanted me to build with had anything to do with why the building was so square, like a big white building block. As usual, I connected what was happening with my visual impressions. On the paper I had been given, the pattern of the blocks was also surrounded by a square, this one drawn with dotted lines. What could this mean? I hadn't seen a dotted square before. I had seen dots before, but only solid drawn squares. Had this new kind of square anything to do with the building and the blocks? My mind did everything it could to find a connection and understand what was happening.

When, after several tests, I was led out of that room and saw my mother at the end of the corridor, I was very confused. I had quite resigned myself to never seeing her again. I had moved into this box. The world seemed to be mocking me, somehow, allowing me to expend so much energy on trying to understand the squares and then—whoosh—taking away the square place. I never went back to that school, and it was a long time before I saw a square drawn with dotted lines again.

My mother said I was driving her mad. My eating habits, my ideas, they were driving her mad. I would say I wanted something, and then refuse to eat it. But I didn't understand. I could answer yes to her question without at all grasping what consequences that might have. My attitude to questions was quite concrete. 'Can you . . . ?' I answered with a 'Yes', which meant 'Yes, I can . . .' But that it should also mean 'I will . . .' or 'I shall . . .' was a totally alien concept to me. If I said 'I can', then I meant just that and nothing else. So the effect of my 'Yes' to the question 'Can you tidy your room?' was not the required one. I didn't at all understand why they were then so cross with me. It seemed that I ought to have understood something that I didn't understand. Sometimes, when I heard quite clearly that the person wanted a special answer, I thought it was good to know what they wanted to hear and so would give them that answer—but without understanding that my answer would perhaps have consequences later.

I moved in the present, and my present consisted of different compartments that had nothing to do with each other, either now or later. It could thoroughly confuse me if a 'then' from one compartment suddenly intervened in a 'now' in another one. It then cost me hours and hours of working out to understand how it had happened. Alternatively, if it was beyond me, I ignored it completely. I excluded it from my system—I couldn't understand it, so it couldn't have anything to do with me, and so it *had* nothing to do with me. Therefore I might, in the eyes of adults, shamelessly and quite insolently look straight through them and not listen when they told me off. But

I didn't feel the insolence they saw. I was simply excluding them from my world.

Kerstin went to jazz-ballet, and I often went with my mother to watch Kerstin practising. I thought it looked fun, not so disorganised and confusing as at playschool. They all stood in their right places and did the same things. There was a class for younger children too, and mother wanted me to start with them. But at first I didn't know if I wanted to, because once before, after seeing a ballet on television and saying that I would like to do that too, I had joined a ballet class for small children but hadn't been able to do the things the ballet teacher told us to do. Everything had been the wrong way round and silly, and I had refused to go back again.

My mother very much wanted me to have other interests, and persuaded me to start jazz-ballet. She talked about what fun it would be. As always, I thought that meant she *knew* it was fun, and that she knew the future in some strange way. She said so. 'It'll be great fun, you'll see,' she said.

So it was decided I should enrol at the dancing class. The first time, I sat right at the front and we did some movements. Then the dancing-teacher came up to me and said my body was unusually supple. 'Like spaghetti,' she said, and it sounded like something good.

I wondered how I could be like spaghetti, but concluded all the same that it must be good to be like spaghetti. I liked spaghetti. But it was not enough to be spaghetti. To be able to dance, it was necessary to be able to follow instructions and to know where you had your arms and legs. I could do neither. My body was indeed very supple and soft, but I couldn't really feel where the various parts of it were, or where they were in relation to each other. I tried to keep up, but when it became totally impossible, when the others did movements I hadn't even the slightest idea which end I should begin with to imitate, I did more or less what I liked. I waved an arm or a leg about in a way that I thought fitted in with the music. You weren't supposed to do that. I had to give it up, as the dancing-teacher said I was disturbing the class.

What was it about me that made the most benevolent and kindly adults after a while get red patches on their necks and be sort of spiky and sharp? I could not make it out.

Seven

School. They had said everything would be better when I started school. I had heard that so many times, I thought they knew it would be. I thought a lot of what had been so difficult, peculiar and incomprehensible was to do with the fact that I didn't go to school, but that everything would simply fall into place once I got there—as if it was some kind of law of nature. So I really did want to go to school. My sister had said some things about it that sounded interesting, and I very much wanted to be a big girl and understand more. So perhaps I now would. They had also said that I would make friends when I went to school.

'You'll make new friends when you go to school'—said so precisely and exactly, like a prediction. I thought they knew.

I was still not particularly interested in other children, but theoretically I wanted to have friends. It sounded as if I ought to want them, like something they thought I would want to have. Kerstin went to school and had friends and I wanted to be like her. However, the result of going to school was not making friends—but a huge shock. If twenty-five children at playschool had overwhelmed me, now there were two hundred and fifty cluttering up my mind. Two hundred and fifty unpredictable voices, and all those arms and legs. Two hundred and fifty bodies to try to make way for. It was physically difficult for me to make way for people. I often walked straight into them, or stopped because I was incapable of calculating my distance from them. I measured and thought and tried to avoid colliding with others. I didn't know how they were able to make way for others. I didn't know that they didn't have to think out what to do, that they simply automatically made way.

All these children at school seemed to be so many millions of empty faces fluttering past before I had time to catch a glimpse and fix my eyes on anything. They did seem to have something to do with each other. I tried to work out the connection between them, but could establish no working theory. One thing I did know, anyway, and that was that none of it had anything to do with me. The teaching at school was also a disappointment. The other children seemed rather stupid. They knew practically nothing and were unable either to read or write. But it was quite pleasant, if boring, to spend my first year at the back of the class playing on my own a game involving a green or red light coming on whenever I read and answered a question. That was what you had to do, to signal whether or not you already knew what the teacher was telling you. Of all the horrible things at school, at least the classroom was the calmest place.

I gradually learnt the names of most of the children in my class, but in the playground I didn't recognise those same children. There were too many faces, merging with each other. They dissolved, their contours blurred and I couldn't keep them apart. I didn't know who was who. The breaks were the worst ordeals of all. Balls would come whistling by from nowhere. A thousand voices. Children running and jumping. It was all one great unpredictable muddle, and it hurt inside whenever I tried to sort out my impressions. I would retreat towards the school building and lean against the wall. I went into myself. Here as well, of course, other children caught the scent of my difference. Perhaps it bewildered them that I was apparently able to behave like a real wet, a silly drip, someone of no significance to whom they didn't have to pay any attention, and yet who at the same time sometimes showed apparently incredible self-confidence and courage, as well as a total indifference to what others thought. I was a drip but I also showed an impressive toughness, and these contradictory features put me in an absolutely special category at school.

I was bullied, so I was one of the group of rejected children. Naturally I was not the only rejected one, and in that group I met with some kind of admiration for my total integrity. If someone had sat on me ten times, I was able to get up and go away as if no one had sat on me at all. In an odd way, I was bullied without being bullied. From the other outsider children's point of view, I seemed tough and strong. In a mysterious way, I could be pushed around *without* being pushed around. It seems impossible, but that's what it was like. I saw admiration in some children's eyes, but I didn't know what use their admiration was.

I also dressed differently. I had a very particular style of my own and had certain favourite clothes that had nothing to do with the standard fashions the other children followed. My clothes were clothes that were visible. An Indian tunic covered with little mirrors and embroidery, an Arab jellaba. A short bright-yellow A-shaped dress with a large zip-fastener that really belonged in the Sixties rather than the Seventies that I was living in—and I also had to have long trousers on under the dress. I had no idea whether it was right to be dressed like this. I liked my clothes enormously, and wearing clothes I liked was very important to me. I was proud of them. I felt good when I was allowed to wear what I thought was beautiful, and I was quite unaware of anyone thinking differently, or whether that was of any importance anyway. This apparent disregard for the conventions contributed to my appearing to be brave. In fact, I had absolutely no idea that there *were* such things as conventions.

My lack of envy could also impress other children, and

make me seem very clever and sensible. I could watch others turning green with envy in certain situations, without any understanding of that emotion. I could certainly covet things, but it never occurred to me to put myself into someone else's place. I never found out how to covet something someone else had, nor had I any desire to *be* anyone else. Generally speaking, my desires were different from those of my girl contemporaries. The three things I most longed for during my childhood were some bagpipes, a tailor's dummy and a microscope. I wanted real things, not toys. But I was hardly ever given what I wanted because adults didn't understand what I wanted such things for. And if they couldn't understand what I wanted them for, then I didn't need them. That was the way their laws worked.

One exception was the microscope, which I had asked for and was actually given, though not until my father had almost destroyed my delight by repeatedly telling me how much I was to use it. He said it wasn't to be left around, and if he was to go to all that expense he certainly wanted to make sure I used it. So at first I was made thoroughly to deserve the microscope by listening to his endless exhortations and then by using it often, to please him. By the time I was given it, after having had it on my list for years, not much of my delight in the instrument was left. But a few years later, the desire to investigate and discover things came back again. I took the microscope out of its red wooden box and went in search of investigation material. Most of what ended up under the lens came from human beings: skin and hair, saliva and nails—anything I could find. My investigations contained a strong desire to find out about human beings. If I could examine things in their most minute detail, perhaps something would be revealed, something would make me understand better, help me to cope with everything.

*   *   *

91

In the playground there were lots of boys who were bigger than me. During one break, some of them came over to me and said they were going to hit me. 'We're going to hit you once a day,' they said.

I thought that a strange rule, but I fell in with it. School was full of things I didn't grasp, and I simply had to comply with them. The boys told me to go with them to the lavatories, which were down in the basement, entered directly from the playground. In there, I was given a punch in the stomach, every day, though usually only one. Perhaps I wasn't much fun to hit because I had a very high pain threshold, and even when it did hurt I never showed what I felt. I didn't know that was what you should do. They hit me every day until someone suddenly told our teacher. I didn't like that. She had nothing to do with me and I thought it insulting. It was now quite clear that I had been deceived in some way, so I felt stupid. Hadn't I gone and found those boys myself, in case on some days they had forgotten to hit me? I had thought that was as it should be.

Now the teacher was going to talk and interfere. I didn't want that. Why couldn't people leave me alone? Those lavatories and the entrance into the playground should be closed, someone said. I didn't understand why I should have caused all this fuss. Those older boys went on hitting me every day behind the school building instead. Once a day. That was safe. I thought it was good when things were the same every day.

I didn't talk like other children, and they didn't always understand what I was saying. I often used difficult words. I might say 'We holidayed in Åland', or 'This is complicated', or 'Do you accept that?' I had no other way of expressing myself and couldn't grasp why they didn't understand. Words came to me easily, as easily as anything. Speech required effort, but the words themselves slid easily into my head and settled in place. Language was clearly inside me, and I liked using the most correct word for each situation.

Turning the words into speech was what was problematical, and meant that I seldom had time to say anything whenever more than two people were involved in a conversation. On paper, on the other hand, words poured out of me. I liked writing and was very good at spelling—in fact I simply couldn't make spelling mistakes. I was almost a dictionary. Having once seen a word in writing, the spelling was stored inside me and I plucked it out whenever I needed it. That talent was not appreciated at school. The teacher thought I was cheating when I got them all right in spelling tests. She talked to me in a kind of understanding, smarmy voice.

'You must see, could it be that . . . I'm not cross with you . . . This is what you do at school.'

A great many long gooey words. Words that said I may be angry now, but I'm a kind person really . . . How could I understand? It was better to be scolded—I could cope with pure anger in adults.

In that teacher's world, you simply couldn't be as good at spelling as I was. The way she saw it, I was afraid of making mistakes, so I looked things up in the book when we had spelling tests. But the fact was that I would never even have dreamt of cheating. I always obeyed the rules made for me as long as they didn't conflict with my most important needs. And I had no need to look in the book—I knew the words anyway. The teacher told me that it was all right to make mistakes. That was allowed. I didn't understand what she wanted, but so as to please her and be left in peace I started deliberately making spelling mistakes. I used my talent for language to calculate which mistakes would be the most likely—to forget one of the double consonants, confuse 'sleep' and 'slip', or use sh instead of ch. I made an effort to make plausible mistakes, and I varied the number of mistakes between one and three each time. I thought that was just about right.

The rules you lived by in this world were very strange. You had to do it as it wasn't, write 'cheep' when it should be spelt 'cheap'. But the teacher was pleased and I was still top of the class at spelling, so I was left in peace.

Although the classroom was the most tranquil place in school for me, I found it difficult to listen when the teacher was talking. I would slip away into myself and disappear, which meant that I kept being moved around. Did I have hearing difficulties? Could I see properly? How would I know? Anyway, I had to change desks, and was put right at the back. Then I was put up at the front, then in the middle, then right at the back again. But it made no difference wherever I sat. Each position in the classroom brought with it different problems.

For me, sitting right at the back was best, although that wasn't always best for school work. I felt more at ease there, and it was good not having anyone behind me. The whole classroom was, anyway, all wrong for me. The teacher prattling on was a background to other noises in my ears—the rustle of paper, scraping chairs, coughing. I heard everything. The sounds slid in over each other and merged together. I couldn't shut them out and put the teacher's voice in the foreground. If I'd thought what she was saying important and interesting, I would perhaps have been able to sort out the impressions 'manually' in order to listen. But what she was saying was seldom what I wanted to know. I needed to understand the world, and she couldn't help me with that.

I found it hard work trying to sort out all the words. Eva might scrape her chair, so I then moved that sound aside and kept it away from what the teacher was saying. Then Stefan would cough, and I had to put this beside the chair-scraping in a little compartment in my head so that there was still room to hear what the teacher was saying. Then Per would move his paper and Anders would drop his pen. By then I didn't know *what* the teacher was saying. I had quickly to put the pen sound aside and try to find my way back. And in that compartment a light was blinking and ticking all the time! Cars outside—quick, put it into the compartment.

I kept trying to hold up a wall in my head between listening and everything around me so that the two shouldn't get mixed. Every sudden sound meant risking losing hold of the wall. With one 'hand' I held the wall up between the sounds, and with the other I tried to clean out my ear so that no new rubbishy sounds got in the way of what I was trying to listen to. With my third 'hand', the one I almost didn't have, I tried at the same time to sort out the information, the content of what I was listening to. This required total concentration, but no one could see what an effort it was. The fact that on certain occasions I was actually able to listen seemed to emphasise the adults' theory that it was only laziness and disinclination on my part that made me often hear nothing at all.

'You can if you really want to.'

Want to? I couldn't find any more 'want to' in me than I was already making use of. I didn't know what they meant. What did they really want of me? I lived on the very edge of what I could cope with, what I could endure. Why did they keep burdening me with more?

I simply couldn't learn to find my way around the school. I thought everything looked the same and I never knew which floor our classroom was on. I often got lost. It was awful arriving late, opening the wrong classroom door and seeing all those vacant faces staring at me. The teacher in the class I'd happened to go into might then quite kindly explain where my classroom was—a long explanation in several stages, which I didn't take in. Of course I knew all the concepts such as 'above' and 'opposite', but I always had to connect them with my visual impressions if they were to be meaningful on any particular occasion. I might well open three more doors before I found the right one. I started going to school extremely early in the mornings so as not to risk arriving late.

In the second grade, the pupils were often given a special assignment. Two eight-year-olds were designated to fetch the lunch for the school dentists. Every term, a draw was held for which class and which pupils were to be given this task, and in the spring term my name and another girl's came up. We were to fetch the lunches from the dining-room, take them to the larger school building a little way away, and leave them at the dental reception there. We were often given a small sum for our trouble. I agreed to this assignment because I usually did what I was told; and money was good to have, I knew that. We went there every day until the day when the other girl in my class was ill. She had always gone with me before.

The teacher told me to go anyway. I could do it on my own. But I couldn't find my way. I couldn't even find my way to the dining-room where I was to collect the lunches, not to mention finding the dental reception place. When I went to our dining-room for school dinner, I always went with the others. I tried to say that I couldn't go on my own because I couldn't find my way. But the teacher told me not to be silly, of course I could. Hadn't I gone that way a hundred times before? Again I tried to explain that I really couldn't. 'Don't be silly,' said the teacher again.

That led me to develop another strategy. I said nothing more, but waited until it was nearly time for the dinner break. Then I went to the teacher and said that I wasn't feeling well, I had a stomach ache. I was allowed to go home. To tell it as it wasn't, that was the solution. I used my intellect and my creativity to give the adults a version that accorded with their view of the world. So in this way, I didn't feel well and had a stomach ache many a time during my schooldays. It meant that if others ever felt sorry for me it was always for something other than what I was really suffering from.

Eight

My mother thought I had calmed down after starting school. I had fewer tantrums, carried out fewer rituals. This was largely because I was exhausted—school took up all my energies. It drained me, and I hadn't even the strength to feel as much terror as I had before, so I became increasingly indifferent. But it was also partly because I had actually matured, and suddenly understood some things I had never previously grasped.

I discovered behind and inside.

It was an enormous discovery, with equal parts of joy and pain, and it completely took my breath away. I was seven, maybe eight, and it was spring or early summer and fairly warm. I was out in the garden tickling the neighbour's cat with a piece of grass. I was wearing my striped dress. The cat, who was called Higgins, was lying almost in the hedge on the neighbour's garden side. I had to reach in among the leaves and twigs to get to him. I looked up, and I saw the hedge separating our garden from the neighbour's; then I looked out over the whole area. As our house was at the top of the hill, I could see a long way, and I glimpsed far off a large handsome house like a palace. It was the old people's home, I'd heard someone say. I saw the houses and the trees, and suddenly light dawned.

There's something behind everything!

I at once knew how things were inside as well, and that this too applied to everything.

Everything has an inside!

The joy of understanding was tremendous. It almost

sang in me, but it also hurt to realise that I hadn't understood before, and that this was something which of course was absolutely obvious to everyone else. I wanted to tell someone, but I had no words with which to explain, and I knew no one would understand if I tried to tell them about my discovery. It also became painfully evident that I could think much more clearly than I could express myself, so I felt very lonely in my great moment.

I was bullied, usually on my way home from school. Children would take my schoolbag and run off with it, or they would yell at me. From the beginning, this was not directed just at me, for all of us in the first grade were teased by the older children. But my different way of reacting seemed to make me the most interesting one to go on bullying. When they took my cap, I just went on home. What did I care about my cap? I didn't like it, anyway. If they took my schoolbag, which I needed, I just stood there and waited. I didn't run after them. I didn't start crying. My lack of reaction seemed to drive them on, but I carried on waiting until they had finished doing what they were doing.

I didn't know who they were, the boys who were nasty to me on my way back from school. I didn't recognise them. They had empty boy faces that simply flowed into each other. I thought they were different boys each time. I didn't know it was a question of my finding it difficult to recognise people. I wondered how these boys, whom I had never seen before, could possibly know that I was the one they were to bully. Did I look peculiar in some way? Had I any special characteristics? Something only they could see? How otherwise could it be that it was just my bag they took and not the other children's, the children who were walking ahead along the road?

I was on my way home from school one afternoon when I was stopped by a fair-haired boy. It was early on in the winter, and everything was covered with a thin layer of snow. The boy stopped me on the space in front of the old fire station and stood facing me, his friends all around him.

'I'm going to rub snow into your face,' he announced.

He said it as if it was inevitable, already decided. He looked at me. I couldn't make out what that look signalled, nor what his body language was saying. He had said he was going to rub snow into my face.

I replied just as I felt. 'Oh yes.' Neither cockily nor submissively. Just verifying it.

He threw me face down on the ground and sat on my back, and I just let him do it. In its submissiveness, my body was saying 'Oh yes' just as I had uttered it, the 'Oh yes' I felt. I was just complying with what he had said he was going to do.

The fair-haired boy was wearing leather gloves. He filled his hands with snow and rubbed my face hard, several times. I let it happen and just waited. After a while, he got up and the weight on my back lifted. I got up, too. I felt neither flattened nor crushed, only miserable that I didn't understand all the strange things that happened in the world. But I didn't let my misery show on the outside. When I looked up at him, I saw his expression change. I hadn't understood the expression I had first seen there, before he had rubbed the snow into my face, but I recognised this one—I saw terror in his face. But I didn't know where it had come from.

His friends ran away. He stared at me and then stammered: 'Go on! Go home! You must go home.'

He picked up my schoolbag and my cap and handed them to me. 'Here! Go on home.'

I looked down at myself. I saw my jacket and trousers were dirty and wet, but I couldn't see what had frightened him so. He gave me a push to make me start going home, then ran away in the other direction. I was bewildered.

Not until I got home did I see that my face was criss-crossed and bleeding from thousands of little scratches. The snow he had rubbed into my face had been filled with little bits of gravel, but with my high pain threshold I hadn't felt it. I had a network of scratches on my cheeks and chin, and the skin on my nose was almost rubbed off. I stood in front of the mirror for a long time, looking at my face. I thought it looked interesting. But I was unhappy, too. Not so much from the actual bullying, or because of the scratches. I was unhappy because I didn't understand, because the world was so unpredictable, so insecure and so lacking in context.

Showing what I felt was a decisive act. It was as if I had to take my feelings, manually, out of myself and turn them into something that could be shown on the outside. I didn't really understand why one should do that. By themselves, my feelings didn't emerge, and I seldom had enough energy to get hold of a feeling and pull it down like a blind in front of me with a message for other people. I had no idea it was important whether other people could or couldn't see what I felt. But that I didn't start crying when I was hit or snow was rubbed into my face was not always simply because I didn't show my misery on the outside. Very often, I wasn't miserable until afterwards. When it was actually happening, I just tried to grasp *what* was happening and why.

My feeling was special in other areas as well, apart from that of pain. I could never take a shower, because I couldn't stand drops of water on my skin. They hurt. They had sharp little points that stabbed me. All forms of washing had to happen in the bath. It was necessary to have as much water around me and all over my body as possible for it to be bearable. I had no special hygiene sense and I would have preferred not to have to wash at all. The vague sense of my body I did have meant that I wasn't particularly aware of whether I was dirty, of the way my clothes were sitting. I didn't feel it. Yet they saw to it that I was fairly clean, and I washed because I was made to. Although I didn't like the actual washing, I liked having a bath. I liked being in water. Water was my element. I felt more at home there, and less clumsy. They said I was like a seal in water. I would have preferred to be that, a seal. Better than being a human being.

At eight, I became over-sensitive to combs and hair-brushes, and I refused to have my hair done. Suddenly, I couldn't bear the pain that came from having my hair done. It seemed to burn like synthetic fire all over my head and the nape of my neck. In some remarkable way, my actual hair seemed to hurt, a pain I also felt inside my ears. I flatly refused, and no attempts by my mother could change it. I was able to resist any threat or bribe.

But although I refused to have it done afterwards, my hair was washed. It dried into a great tangled mass and then stayed like that. When my hair wasn't done properly, it seemed to reach a certain stage of unruliness and then stop there. As if it had its own limit for how tangled it could be.

No one could prevail upon me. I would run away, scream, bite, scratch and claw—I would do anything. How-ever far an adult was prepared to go to make me, I was always ready to go one step further. It was my terror that drove me, but they couldn't understand why the wretched child was so stubborn.

'For heaven's sake, surely you can stand a bit of pulling? If you want to look nice, you have to put up with a bit of hurt.'

But the whole of me would be one great No. Other people, when they didn't want to do something, always seemed to have a little 'yes' or 'perhaps' tucked away somewhere. I exuded No through every pore. There was nothing else, only me and No, united and impregnable, with not the merest chance of anyone breaking in.

I sensed that my behaviour made my mother feel a failure, but I couldn't make out how or why. The colour of her sense of failure as a mother was sulphurous, yellowish. That yellow colour, mixed with my sense of constantly disappointing other people, ended up in a compartment for guilty conscience in my stomach. My mother also sent ambiguous messages, which made everything even more difficult. She wanted to get through to me and felt she had failed as a mother because she couldn't. On the other hand, her ego occasionally glinted, purple, frustrated over my not loving her. Then in desperation, via ingratiation or slaps, she would try to get me to show her some love. Neither approach gave me any sense that I ought to. My guilty conscience grew worse.

In the second grade, the time came to begin learning the recorder, and I wanted to. I knew nothing about how to play an instrument, but I liked music. Accordion music, bagpipes, and the music to the film *Zorba* were my favourites. Kerstin played the clarinet and had also started to learn the flute in the second grade, so now I was to take over her recorder. The local music school, as it was called, began its courses in the autumn and the teaching took place on school premises. I thought it a good thing to be allowed to stay on at school in the afternoon. It felt important and right to look after the brown recorder bag during the day, and I liked carrying it.

The music teacher was a thin little man with glasses. This surprised me. I thought he didn't fit, because in my strong desire to understand the system by which the world was constructed, I had created a glasses theory. All adults who wore glasses were either tall and thin, or short and fat, I had deduced. Not short and thin. I had based the theory on the appearance of my father and one of his friends at work. I had never before seen anyone who was both short and thin and who also wore glasses. I had never noticed what all those empty faces in the street or in shops looked like, so they played no part in my theories anyway. The music teacher frightened me because he was quite a different kind, one who didn't conform with my experience, and I never knew whether new kinds of people who didn't conform with my theories might prove to be dangerous. Everything unfamiliar was dangerous and made me feel insecure.

I now had my sister's recorder in its case and was truly looking forward to solving the mystery of music. We had to learn to unpack and clean our recorders with a special brush. The music teacher handed out little exercise books, and we had to copy out squiggles into them. I did everything we were supposed to do, and drew as well as I possibly could. But I had no idea what he was talking about. And I didn't really understand that I didn't understand. I thought the situation with the squiggles was much the same as what I had found when learning to read. You look at the squiggles and blow down the recorder so that it sounds just as it is on the paper. It didn't sound at all like it was on the lined paper when I played, but I didn't know that. I tootled away just the same. The music teacher said things to me that I didn't take in. I thought he was being peculiar, almost angry. He asked if I really did want to learn to play the recorder. A strange question, for of course I did. I wanted terribly to learn to play it.

But one evening when my mother came to collect me, he asked her to stay behind until the others had left.

'Impossible . . . I can't have her here.'

I heard him, but I didn't really follow. When my mother told me I couldn't go on playing, I couldn't make out why not. It ended up in my failures compartment, and I never closed that compartment, for then I would have had to keep on opening it.

Kerstin said that the recorder was now hers as I had stopped going to music school, but anyway, I considered it mine. I couldn't play, but I liked cleaning it with that brush that belonged to it, and often did so. It fascinated me that such a big brush could go through that small opening. In the same way as I needed curved things, I could sometimes need things that fitted exactly into each other. It calmed me when something fitted exactly into something else. I didn't like large spaces in between. I wanted it to touch on all sides equally, from all directions. It was the same feeling that meant that I usually found myself under or in between things. I wanted either that everything should be a large space, a vacuum, around me, or that there should be no spaces at all.

It was preferable if it was absolutely tight all round me, and at sleep time it was best if I could get father to fold the mattress round me, then fasten the sheet firmly around it so that I was lying in a tight roll of mattress. But at home there wasn't always someone available who would agree to do as I wanted, or who had time to. They all had so much to squabble about. But regardless of how I was lying in bed, there was always one way of getting to sleep, and that was to toss my head to and fro on the pillow, from side to side, very quickly. This was the only way to fall asleep. In the daytime, I could just shut out the world, sink into myself and switch off wakefulness without falling asleep. So in order to be able to get past that place in which wakefulness was switched off but sleep not yet switched on, I had to find another method of falling asleep. My method worked well, although occasionally I had to keep tossing my head to and fro quite violently for a long time.

Nine

Aunt Berit was a woman who lived in the neighbourhood and had two daughters, one of them, Camilla, a year younger than me. We were considered contemporaries. My parents were not exactly good friends with Aunt Berit and her husband, but they were acquaintances and they found it convenient to child-mind for each other. Camilla had been looked after by us for a while, when I was three. At the time, I had been uncertain as to whether she belonged in our family, whether she was perhaps a new sister. She had seemed very odd when she used to hang on the gate and scream for her mother. I had found her behaviour unfathomable. I had never screamed for my mother. Why should anyone do that?

I knew now she didn't belong in our family. I considered her a boring cry-baby, a cry-baby I had to put up with when I sometimes had to go there after school. It had been decided that I was to go to Aunt Berit's on certain days of the week and be given something to eat, as my mother couldn't be at home at those times. Although Camilla was boring, I could bear that, but her mother became my tormentor. Aunt Berit was a live version of the bossy Prusseluska, like the one in the Pippi Longstocking books, but without her comical side. She thought that I 'ought to know better'. I turned this comment over and over, but could detect no meaning in it. *What* ought I to know? If I asked, she snapped back at me not to be insolent. I didn't like her, and—as she had quite rightly often noticed—I had no particular respect for her. On the other hand, she considered she liked me, or at least cared for me, and seemed to see it as her lifetime's task to improve my manners according to her lights. Aunt Berit believed that it would be a charitable deed on her part if she were to make me the object of some of her child-rearing methods, and I ought to appreciate that.

I once bit Aunt Berit. This happened one day when I was placed in her care because my family was to be away for twenty-four hours. Cross with me for something I had done, she made one of her attempts at teaching me manners. She took hold of me and shook me hard—it was horribly unpleasant, and I felt violated. Adults in general had nothing to do with me, especially Aunt Berit. I had to make her let go of me, so I leant over the hand holding and shaking me and then bit it—hard.

I would never again allow her to insult me. Never. What made her think she had the right to take hold of me like that? I was me, and she didn't belong in my world, because I didn't know her well and I didn't like her. She was not to be permitted to interfere in my world and manhandle me. This was quite simply not an option. Never was she to be allowed to mess me about again, ever.

Aunt Berit screamed and let go of me, and the moment she did, I ran. I ran off, out through the front door, with no shoes or jacket on. I ran in my stockinged feet down their garden and out on to the street, Aunt Berit chasing after me. I wasn't really fast enough, but I had a firm conviction that I had to get away from there, had to be left in peace—a conviction that gave me strength. I also knew which gardens I could take a short cut through to get home, and Aunt Berit wasn't the kind of woman to take short cuts through other people's gardens whether she knew the way or not. So I got there before her.

She knew I hadn't planned to run away and she knew I hadn't any keys to get in at home, so she thought she would catch me on the way. But I knew something she didn't know—that you could break a pane in our basement window, put your hand through and open the catch from the inside. Then you could get up into the hall via the basement stairs, and you were there. So I could get into our house without a key. I was already inside, standing at the hall window by the front door, when I saw her come panting through the gate and up the path to the house. I was pleased she couldn't get at me as I watched her from the window. Never, never would I let her in, never would she be allowed anywhere near me.

Aunt Berit stood outside and shouted at me through the window, both angrily and appealingly. She was apologising. I stood inside and watched her. Apologies had no intelligible content in my world. You did what you did. I simply couldn't imagine that you could do and say things you didn't mean and then say you were sorry. I meant exactly what I said and did. Aunt Berit shouted even louder. Presumably she thought I couldn't hear through the window.

'Open the door!' she cried.

I couldn't actually do that, because I had no key. I just stared at her through the window without answering. In the end, she had to give up and go home. It was nice when she left, though it was peculiar being alone in the house. The telephone rang several times and at first I didn't answer, but when I finally did, of course it was Aunt Berit. I was frightened of her now and could say nothing but 'No' into the receiver, whatever she said. 'No, no, no.'

Aunt Berit didn't sound all that angry, but then she declared that I was impossible and began to threaten me, saying she would certainly see what my parents had to say about my behaviour. Then she rang off. A moment later, the phone rang again. This time it was my parents. They had talked to Aunt Berit, but they said I could stay at home on my own if I wanted to. This was a relief. They hadn't told her how to get into the house and I was being allowed to stay at home by myself. This was one of the few times I felt they were on my side, that they approved of my action.

It was also the first and only time I ever spent a night quite alone at home. For once I would be able to turn on every single light in the entire house before going to bed, without anyone stopping me. What made the dark so horrible was that it blinded me, because my eyes never got used to it. As it grew darker, everything just got greyer until it was like looking at the television when the programmes were over—a kind of gravelly grey darkness that made me lose all sense of direction. I went through the whole house and switched on all the lights. Of course, I was never permitted to do that usually. Wanting all the lights on was a silly idea, and a waste of electricity.

Aunt Berit did not like me, and I knew she didn't. Why, then, didn't she leave me alone? Why did she say the opposite of how it was? 'For your own good . . . because I'm fond of you . . . because I wish you well . . .'—that was what she *said*. But what I actually felt was that she thought I was a horrid, lazy, ill-mannered brat.

My mother's sense of what was really appropriate had begun to deteriorate at the same rate as her doctor prescribed her Valium. I was eight and a half now, and Aunt Berit's Camilla was almost seven. I was invited to her party, one of the few parties I had ever been invited to; and to make me look my best, Mamma painted my lips with lipstick before I went. I didn't know anything about looking my best for a party—it was her idea entirely. Furthermore, I had never felt tempted by such ladyish accessories as make-up, dresses and high-heeled shoes. And of course, I couldn't bear jewellery. I did occasionally dress up in my grandmother's silk frock when Kerstin was trying on Mamma's wedding dress, but that wasn't something I would have thought up myself. I had neither the desire nor the motivation to be a princess. I just wanted whatever I perceived Kerstin wanted. I didn't know what it was—I just saw the colour of her feelings. I saw something pale blue in her, I saw that she wanted to look grand, to try on adult clothes with lots of lace on them. I didn't understand, and would never have been able to guess that the point was that I would become an adult, that I would be the same sort as my parents. I'd agreed to the lipstick because, despite everything, my mother seemed to know more about parties than I did. But it turned out that she didn't know anything about how you should look at parties.

Aunt Berit and her family were free-thinkers. When I arrived at the birthday party, she told me to go and wash off the lipstick. I refused, not because I wanted to keep the lipstick on, but more because I didn't want her making decisions for me. When the cake had been eaten and it was time to go and play, I retreated into myself. I didn't know the other children. They were Camilla's friends and they were all younger than me. They played doctors in Camilla's room, examining each others sexual parts, but as that didn't interest me any more than other group games did, I went and sat under a table.

The table I was under was covered with a large piece of cloth that hung down the sides so that it became a cabin inside. The cloth had in fact been made up into a cabin, and there were plastic windows in it. I liked being there. After a while, Camilla's younger sister came into the cabin and sat down. She was only three, and too young to think it exciting to play at doctors. She played with the dolls, and I just sat there, absorbed in myself.

Suddenly I heard shrieks and other loud noises from the room, and the little sister and I emerged from the cabin. Aunt Berit was standing in the doorway, agitated and red in the face. I had never seen her like this before. She strode straight over to me and grabbed me by the ear, then dragged me down the stairs. I was in a state of shock, could comprehend nothing.

'Just look what kind of a girl *you* are! With a face like that! So cheap!'

She was gripping the back of my neck tightly with one hand, and with the other rubbing my mouth hard so as to smear the lipstick all over my face. I was quite horrible to lure her children into such games, she said, and now I would be answerable to the other children's parents. I couldn't make it out. I had never seen an adult behave in this way before. It was incomprehensible, and I was so shocked, I just complied with what was happening. With her hand firmly grasping my neck—I was certainly not going to run away this time—she phoned the other children's parents. When they came to fetch them, she tried to make me say I was sorry to them all, one by one, but unsuccessfully. By that stage, the whole situation had become insuperable, and I had shut the world out and gone into myself. I stood mutely in her hall looking straight through the worried parents who had arrived to collect their offspring, while Aunt Berit told her story about how awful and lost I was. In the end she let me go, with a warning about how angry my parents would be when she told them. The strange thing was, they didn't react at all, and that made the whole affair even more unfathomable. 'Oh, yes? Really? Then we'll go home, shall we?' was all they said. Aunt Berit looked odd, and I didn't know whether to be pleased or miserable that her predictions of dire punishment hadn't materialised. I felt just confused and wretched.

I made a mental note of two things, two things that seemed to me to be some kind of key to ever understanding what had happened: it could be seen on me what kind of person I was—and the word 'lost'. Lost. Had my peculiarities something to do with my having lost something, or someone having lost *me*? When I was small, perhaps? And what was it they could see on me that I couldn't see in the mirror? It must be *something*. She'd just said so.

This also fitted in well with what those boys who had taken my bag on the way home from school had said. It must be the reason why they knew it was my bag in particular they were to take. It was because something showed on me. But what?

Not until long after, as an adult, and after having come across various Aunt Berits, did I begin to grasp a little of what had happened at that party. And then I realised that what made me end up wholly in the power of people like that was that I didn't recognise that mixture of anger and pleasure, that desire to do something at someone else's expense. I had never felt like that, and couldn't work out what it was I could see in other people's faces.

Other people, even those who didn't live out their emotions in this way, seemed to be able to recognise and understand it all, and to know what to watch out for. I didn't know that. I didn't mingle sufficiently with people for it even to enter my head to begrudge anyone anything, or to wish anyone ill. I never took things personally in the way that others seemed to, and I had no sense of having any prestige to lose. I never felt provoked. I didn't even understand that there was such a feeling, even less that I could arouse it in others. The basic emotional states, sorrow and joy, did of course exist in me, but I didn't take them out into the world and glue them on to other people. So I couldn't recognise those complex emotions shown by others.

I was defenceless when faced with people's calculated malice, because I didn't understand it. I did have experience of my father, who was often both malicious and violent—which could be mortally dangerous. But that experience was not enough to permit me to grasp what was going on, because his malice was more a kind of stupid spite. Of course, he was manipulative, and he would alter reality according to his own needs, but there was something cold, empty and stupid about him. He had none of

that sharp-beaked, pointed malice, that calculated malevolence that Aunt Berit had. I didn't know what attitude
to take to that kind of person—the sort who thought they
had the right to humiliate others according to their own
lights, the sort who claimed to be your friend when in
fact they were your enemy. Pia and Aunt Berit were my
first experiences of this, and it was so utterly alien to me
that I was totally at their mercy.

Junior school work went well. I already knew most of it,
and that meant I seemed to be clever even at what didn't
go so well. Kerstin had been at the same school before
me, and everyone expected me to be clever sister number
two. Gymnastics was the major exception, as everything
about it frightened me. I was terrified of being pushed or
of seeing a ball hurtling towards me. I knew without a
shadow of a doubt that I couldn't rely either on my body
or on my senses, and that it really was logical to be scared
to death of the apparatus. But there was no one who could
understand.

At a certain age we were supposed to be able to turn
somersaults, and I was the only one who couldn't. When
I got on all fours and put my head down, all sense of
space, direction and body simply vanished. I tried my usual
method of dealing with life's difficulties—I refused. But
it turned out to be more difficult at school than at home.
It was hard to be a step ahead when confronted with all
those empty faces, and as usual I was unable to work out
how people would react.

In the end, it was decided that I was to practise somersaults at home. I sat at the end of my parents' double bed,
and tried to gather enough courage just to put my head
down and turn the world upside down. One step at a time.
Several times, I got on all fours with my head down at the
foot of the bed, and turned terribly dizzy without even
daring to let go. I couldn't believe it was worth all the

trouble. I had no use whatsoever for turning somersaults. When I did finally dare let go and roll over, it was a ghastly experience. I was thrown straight out into space. My sensory faculties were unable to follow the movement and it was just indescribably terrible, as if someone had turned the room I was in upside down and shaken it. Nothing would ever make me do it again. No one would force me to repeat that. Now I had the strength to refuse point-blank, a strength generated out of sheer panic.

I became an impossible child when it came to gymnastics. I couldn't climb up the wall bars, as I immediately suffered from vertigo. I never twigged the rules of ball games, and was never able to judge the speed of the ball sufficiently well to catch it. I could never make out why year in and year out I was made to take gymnastics, which was nothing but a torment. Nor could I understand what school really was, what it was for. It seemed to have been devised as a personal instrument of torture, for me. The confusion and the presence of other children multiplied all my symptoms many times over, and if anyone had asked me what was the point of school, I wouldn't have been able to answer. I had no idea.

In the third grade, we started woodwork. This was the Seventies and the new age, so the girls were to do woodwork and the boys needlework. I ended up in the half of the class that was to start woodwork. I had begun to learn that free expression, doing what *I* liked, was not appreciated at school, so I'd become more and more exhausted and dejected. I didn't understand verbal instructions, which meant woodwork lessons were a disaster. The woodwork master kept explaining, but I didn't understand. Making three-dimensional hollow things did not suit my detailed little two-dimensional vision. I did nothing whatsoever, just hung over the bench or looked out of the window. At first it went well enough, just living through the lessons and hoping he would leave me alone. It suited me fine to do nothing. But then we were supposed to begin using the machines, the big lathe and the band-saw.

Before I had started woodwork, the sounds that had disturbed me at school had been the mumbling, scraping and shouting kind, the kind I heard every single component of and could not shut out, as they settled like a thick carpet on my mind. But now these machines came into my life, and with their din pulled the world from under my feet. I would press my hands to my ears when they started up, but nearly always too late. It hurt inside me, and I kept on and on losing all sense of direction and of myself.

When the teacher tried to get me to use the saw to learn how to work it, I backed away and ran out into the playground—an entirely healthy instinct, one of self-preservation. Who would voluntarily stand by a band-saw, with hands near the blade, and lose the feeling of where their body was? But in the eyes of everyone around, there was no such logic. Now I was being troublesome again, for no reason at all. But I felt I really wouldn't survive those noises once a week. I felt it so strongly that I managed to be ill every Wednesday when we were to have woodwork. If necessary, panic would bring on a temperature, and I had to stay at home. Eventually it became all too obvious that I was ill only on Wednesdays, so then I took to a less sophisticated method. I quite simply refused to go to woodwork. I was an immovable rock of intransigence.

This led to discussions between my mother, the school and the woodwork master about, as they thought, my fear of using machinery. No one could imagine that it was the actual noise, whether it was me or anyone else who was operating the machine, that so tormented me. Would I consider going if I didn't have to use the saw?

'No.'

'If . . .'

'No.'

'You must go to the lessons!'

'No.'

My mother didn't actually know the reason, but she did grasp the seriousness of my protests, so she took the matter further up the school hierarchy. In the end I was excused woodwork, actually excused it for ever. At least I had escaped *one* torment, and it was a relief to be allowed to sit in the light, quiet and concentrated space of the needlework room.

'Why is she allowed to?'

'Why just her?'

'How unfair!'

I heard all their comments, but ignored them. It was unfair, of course, and there was sure to be someone else who also wanted to get out of woodwork for one reason or another.

I was pleased, even if my inability to understand verbal instructions also became clear in needlework lessons— my knitted snake consisted of more holes than stitches. But anyway, I was good with a needle and thread, pernickety things suited my good vision, and it was easy to use my fingers at precision work when I had plenty of time and calm all around me.

Some time during the third grade, the realisation that I was different began to grow. The discovery of behind and inside became a kind of awakening that made me see myself more clearly in relation to the world around. Why were things that seemed easy to other people so difficult for me? Was I perhaps backward? But without having realised it myself? Was it that people didn't want to tell me I was backward? What was wrong with me? Why wasn't I a real person?

I sank into a sense of pointlessness, began comfort eating and grew fat. Now at least I had an externally tangible feature to be teased about. Fatty. This was painful and I didn't want to be fat, but nonetheless it was a lesser evil than the evil of being bullied for something I didn't recognise. I also discovered how easily deceived I had been before, though I felt no self-pity. I must have been quite mindlessly foolish and dumb to have agreed to so much that other children had exposed me to. I realised now, on a kind of inkling level, without grasping the whole problem, that I didn't really understand people's intentions. I couldn't read in their faces and bodies whether they were stupid or kind, friend or foe. And their actions were often so confusing that they too were unable to help me to work out whether people wished me well or ill. So I now became extremely suspicious of everyone, and sensitive about making a fool of myself. I came to the conclusion that in all situations it was better to do nothing than make mistakes.

When I was smaller, I had occasionally approached people, if in a rather intrusive manner. I had usually wanted to be left to my own devices, in peace, but if I thought it was OK to sit on someone's lap, it didn't matter whose lap it was. Sitting on the lap of a stranger, on the lap of an empty face, hadn't been any more difficult than sitting on an armchair. In fact, those empty faces were almost like furniture. I wasn't as shy and anxious as Kerstin at that time; whenever I wasn't enclosed in myself, I had a kind of straightforwardness devoid of all respect. This lack of respect was healthier and more vital than the suspicious introversion that now took its place.

I had previously found it difficult to generalise, and to apply an experience from one area of life to another. I now began to generalise exaggeratedly. I deduced that as behind and inside applied to everything, this was sure to be where the centre of understanding was. It was a matter of taking with you what you knew. The compartments were not separate. Everything went together. What happened here could also happen there. It was important to try to maintain a thread from one situation to another. This soon became more than theory—it became a truth that would have consequences for my way of trying to understand the world in the future.

In the world out there were lavatories, and at home we had two, one on the upper floor and the other on the ground floor of our house. There was nothing strange about this, that's how it was—one lavatory upstairs and another downstairs. But then I had noticed that in some places there were two lavatories together, alongside each other, and that one was for boys and the other for girls. I had also grasped that there were two kinds of places in the world. There was 'someone's home' and then there was 'not someone's home'. This was crystal-clear to me and I had no idea that other people divided up the world into more places. Where there were two lavatories together, one for boys and the other for girls, was in those places that were not someone's home. In all the places in the world that *were* someone's home, the lavatories were always single.

School was not home for anyone, and on the same floor as our classroom in middle school there were two lavatories, wall to wall. So one had to be for boys and the other for girls. But there was nothing on them, and I tried to deduce how I could find out which was the one for girls. There *must* be a sign of some sort on the doors, because the others didn't hesitate over where they should go.

I studied the doors very carefully so as to find what the others seemed to see, but I didn't. I had a fleeting thought that maybe the others knew automatically which lavatory they should go into, and so needed no special labels in the way I did. Perhaps they had innate abilities for knowing that kind of thing? In a way, this idea was nearest to the truth, but to me it seemed unlikely all the same. It was too mysterious for my concrete mind that they should just *know*. Also, it would have made me give up completely—if the others knew things like this automatically, there was no point in me even trying to sort it out.

On the floor below our classroom, there was a single lavatory in the corridor. According to my concrete logic, that one must be for the use of both boys and girls. But I couldn't go there at break. And they would all wonder why I didn't go to the nearest lavatories. So I had to go there during lesson time. I didn't like doing that, though, because you had to ask the teacher for permission, but it was better than risking making a mistake. I worked out ways for how and when and where I would go. With my already low status, I couldn't afford to make a fool of myself in front of my classmates, and it was important to me to follow the clear rules and regulations that existed. I wanted to do the right thing.

At junior level, I'd had problems finding my way back to the classroom after going to the lavatory. Then I'd had to go during break and run the gauntlet of the others, who might wonder why I went down to the single lavatory outside the woodwork room. I did this because it was at ground level just by the stairs, which I could easily find my way to and from. But I couldn't explain this to anyone, as the world outside had already decided that I could find my way everywhere.

At middle school, finding my way about started to get easier. The class had been moved to another building in the same courtyard, and our classroom was up at the top and the furthest away. There was no other classroom on that floor—only a woodwork room and a music room—and they had quite different doors. So now I could at least find my way back.

At break, I tried to see which of the two lavatories outside our classroom the other children used, so that in that way I could work out which was which. But as soon as the class seethed out of the classroom all their faces merged together, and I couldn't tell who was who or who did what. It was as if their individual features wouldn't stick in my mind if I didn't see them in their places in the classroom. I remembered the outlines, the basics, of their appearance—who was dark-haired, who wore glasses and that kind of thing. But when they weren't all quite still in prescribed places, all the dark-haired ones would merge into one. So I went on searching for some form of visible code that would show me which lavatory was for girls.

I also had another problem, which required extending my lavatory strategies, though it was a problem I never understood until I was adult. I thought it was the same for everyone. I couldn't feel that I needed to go the lavatory, so I had to think out when I needed to go. I didn't know other people had a signalling system that warned them at intervals before the need to go became urgent. I had no such system. I felt nothing, nothing, nothing . . .— then it was urgent, then I felt it, and then I had to find a lavatory at once. So I always had to go beforehand and very frequently, so that it could never become that urgent.

Ten

There was one game that entailed Kerstin and a friend of hers going down into our basement and dressing up. Then they would come back up into the house and say their names were Sausage Cat and Esmeralda. They were my guardian angels and they loved cats, they said. I believed them and swallowed it all. I hadn't grasped that it was Kerstin and her friend, nor even that it was a game. In my world, it didn't have to be my sister just because she resembled Kerstin. They were wearing quite different clothes and she'd said her name was Esmeralda. I was slightly scared of them, but at the same time it seemed exciting to have guardian angels. They said I could be a guardian angel too, and I wanted to be. I very much wanted to be something different from what I was. I wanted to be something, anything, anything at all that people knew and could recognise.

Perhaps it was both exciting and a little frightening for them too that I actually swallowed it hook, line and sinker, and perhaps they felt that another child of my age wouldn't have done so. But then one day I realised they were deceiving me, and once I had taken in how silly I must have been not to have seen, I began to appreciate the game. I wasn't frightened any longer, and I wanted them to be Sausage Cat and Esmeralda all the time. I went on and on about it, and they didn't think it was fun any longer. I was terribly disappointed that they hardly ever wanted to play Sausage Cat and Esmeralda with me, now that at last I'd twigged. If I did manage to persuade them, I didn't at all mind that they were rather half-hearted and apathetic. I never noticed differences in that kind of thing, anyway. To me, it was perfectly all right if it was exactly the same every time. But the game more or less died out and disappeared the moment I had understood.

I was always trying to make out what was happening around me, and to me, growing older was linked with my desire to understand better. This was why I wanted to be older—this, and a vision I had that when I was grown up I would at last be left in peace. But when I did get to understand something, it would turn out that even more difficulties, new difficulties, came into play. And the older I grew the more was demanded of me, while at the same time I had increasingly less access to any childish charm that might have compensated for my failings. A withdrawn chubby four-year-old could be met with a little more indulgence from the world around her than a suspicious and overweight ten-year-old.

At junior school, the teacher had let me sit and draw on rough paper during lessons, and this had helped me stop sinking into myself. With paper and pen, I could keep my nervous system awake. True, I hadn't listened any more attentively to the lessons, had concentrated more on what I was drawing, but this hadn't mattered because I already knew what was being taught. I didn't know that advantages of this kind were to be suddenly withdrawn, and that now that we had a new teacher in the fourth grade all special treatment had come to an end.

I had to understand that it was not permitted to sit drawing during lesson times.

But as the teacher was talking, a monotonous heaving ocean would well up in my ears, a sea with surging waves of rustling and coughing. It would make me slowly sink into myself and stay there. That inner emptiness was perhaps not all that unlike meditation, but with the great difference that I usually did not control the state myself.

It just happened: my mains supply slumped to zero, then switched off, disconnected.

As I had begun to be aware that something really did distinguish me from the others, it became even more painful to keep disappearing into myself. I kept feeling all the time that I was not living up to the expectations they all had of me. I felt I was disappointing other people, and I really tried to combat it. But they had put me in a situation that acted like ether on my nervous system, while requiring me to be awake, alert, present. They also demanded that I be quiet and sit still. I could use neither my voice nor my body as an aid to keeping me in the room. They might just as well have asked me to stand on my hands and peel oranges. But I believed them when they said I was lazy. Everyone else could sit still and both hear and listen. Then it must be true what they said, although I always fought so hard to be the person they seemed to want me to be. They said 'Be like this!' but they didn't want to give me the equipment to be like it, and I did my best without knowing that there was not a hope in heaven.

Now that I was no longer given any rough paper, I started drawing on my desk. This was strictly forbidden, but I had got so used to having the paper that I was scarcely aware that I was drawing on the desk. It kept me in the here and now, in the room, so that I heard when the teacher addressed me. If on account of some activity or incident I couldn't keep myself present, if I sank into myself, then I never heard if anyone spoke to me. And it was important to answer when spoken to, I knew that. Not answering seemed to be what provoked them most of all. So I tried to remain present—I drew on the desk, was reprimanded, tried to stop drawing on the desk, sank into myself, didn't answer when spoken to, was reprimanded, tried to be present, started drawing on the desk again, and so on.

My achievements in school now also fluctuated. As far as languages, both Swedish and English, were concerned, it was of no importance whether I listened to the lessons or not. I could read and spell perfectly, anyway. It had always been enough for me to see how a word was spelt once for me to remember it. And I was conservatively correct in my use of Swedish. I didn't like the language reforms of the 1970s at all, but went on writing the old forms. I liked the rhythms of the language and very much enjoyed putting in commas and full stops. I was presumably the only pupil to use the semi-colon in my compositions in middle school. Full stops, colons and commas were like musical instruments, I thought. You could play them.

I also read a great deal at home, and I loved Fröding. Poems were like fairy-tales but better, because they had strict rhythms that appealed to my sense of order and my desire for predictability. I wanted to read about pain, suffering and death, and about being an outsider.

> I the ailing linden,
> dying when still young.
> Dead leaves to the wind
> is all my crown can strew—
> Leaves, fall, wind, away!
> Rustling in the leaves on dry brown ground.

> Alone it coils in rings,
> deathly old and tired.
> The lark above doth swing
> hovering on happy wing
> hear it, hear it sing
> the snake may not join in.*

* From the poems 'Give Life and Oblivion' and 'The Song of the Snake', in *Gleanings* by Gustav Fröding.

These poems appealed to my ten-year-old soul. And I could clearly see the colour of Fröding's melancholy, perhaps even more clearly because I did not understand all the dimensions of the words. I didn't take in much of the overall content of the poems—I just ignored bits I didn't understand. But the bits that I alighted on here and there all said something to me, something closer to my reality than anything shown on television, or in all those children's books. It was mostly the actual words, though, that I was looking for. I could leaf back and forth through books and would start reading only when some word caught my interest. I was looking for new and untasted ones. My need for new words that could be discovered and investigated, that would then slip softly into place in my mind, was greater than my need for people. Words aroused my curiosity and a kind of hunger. I always had any amount of space for new ones. 'Vendetta', 'dilettante' . . .—I revelled in them.

For the same reason, I had loved Lennart Hellsing's books when I was younger, because they put croquembouches, coppersmiths and drum-majors into my vocabulary. And Constantineapolitans. Although language, words and rhythm were the essentials, what really captivated me were intimations of rejection and suffering—then I could decipher them. In Victor Rydberg's *Singoalla*, I found passages that told me much more than did the children's programmes on television: 'I must tell you that this dark-eyed woman is a creature of a different species from yours, a child of unfathomable nature . . .—a repudiated creature, a non-Christian, a semi-troll . . .' And: 'The world is a graveyard . . . and my heart is truly dead and buried, no longer able to feel sorrow.'

The child in *Singoalla* called Child of Sorrow suited my desire for a clear and concrete world. You knew what a child of sorrow was. You could hear it in the name. The fact that the book was a love story, on the other hand, completely passed me by. I also read Hans Christian Andersen and *Grimm's Fairy-Tales*, but only the grimmest tales with the cruellest endings—chopped-off feet, children frozen to death, and the unpredictable evil in life. People on whom misfortune falls. I was searching for myself. Perhaps I would suddenly turn the page and find the story of myself there? Sometimes I seemed to be given little hints that this might be so. In *Singoalla* there were hermits. I found out what that meant and felt related to them. Would I be a hermit when I grew up? I was constantly looking for an explanation of what was wrong with me, searching for a purpose in life. The hope of some kind of explanation was always there in my subconscious.

It was this hope, although entirely subconscious, that made me leaf through medical books, looking at pictures of carcinomas—the amazing word for that disease in these books—at boils and genetic malformations. The lessons at school about how the human body functioned aroused my interest then. Although I really had no special difficulty in learning facts, I had begun to slide back in subjects based on knowledge. What was on offer at school was so totally uninteresting. I needed to learn skills, not about how many stomachs a cow had or what the farmers of Sweden produced. Knowledge of that kind said nothing to me and had nothing to do with my world. I needed to learn how you found your way around school, which lavatories to go to, what you did when you played, and how my body worked. Needing, as I did, to learn how to survive my everyday life, how could I take an interest in the Three Wise Men? And yet I was considered to find school work easy, and this was perhaps because what I was good at I was tremendously good at.

I could feel the demands growing. If I was good at this, well then, I ought to be good at that, too. If not, I was lazy and spoilt, and should at once pull myself together. The only thing that really pleased me was being good at drawing. That made no demands. I drew details and perspective with a fine exactitude, and apart from liking drawing myself, my drawings also impressed the other children. But in the eyes of the school, drawing was never a subject that counted. Top marks in drawing was nothing.

The confusion of impressions I experienced during break still tormented me, but I now found it a little easier to have people around me. I had hardly any choice but to try to get used to it. Also, I had made a great effort to get rid of particular characteristics, such as my taste for certain clothes. I wanted to be as little different as possible, so I tried to smooth away and bleach out the stronger parts of my personality. I did do my hair now and it had actually become less sensitive, and I bought the same jeans as everyone else.

I became slightly more accepted at school, but unfortunately this signalled the beginning of a slow change in my view of myself, a kind of poisoning of my self-respect. Previously, when I hadn't thought of myself as a real person, I'd had some sense of belonging, but to a different species. Now I still didn't feel like a real person—rather, a poor imitation of other people, a kind of faulty copy.

I tried asking questions to find out whether there was anything tangibly the matter with me. I had this vague, insistent idea all the time—*that there was something wrong with me.* But questions that to me were deeply serious were answered in amused voices: 'Oh, no, there's nothing wrong with you, dear.'

They probably hadn't understood the question. I had to ask it again, in another way. I tried again: 'Is there something strange about me?'

Smiling voices from above. Voices with joky little gurgles in them. 'Something strange? There's nothing strange about you. Hahaha. Well . . . I suppose you could say you do ask a lot of questions.'

Quite simply, something had to be wrong with people

who could joke about things that were so deadly serious. Or was I wrong? The message I got, the few times I dared try to find out what the situation really was, was that the problem was not that there was anything wrong with me, but that I *thought* there was something wrong with me.

A short while into the autumn term of the fourth grade, a little shed was suddenly put up in the school yard. I saw it there, all bolted and barred for a week or two, then one dinner break it was suddenly open. Several children were crowding round it, and I too gradually made my way over to see what it was. Inside the shed, to my horror, I saw Aunt Berit. In some incomprehensible way she had managed to fly between two worlds and had landed here in my school world. I certainly did not need any more of Aunt Berit in my life. I was still being sent to her on certain afternoons when there was no one at home, and I still disliked her just as much.

I couldn't believe that Aunt Berit could appear in yet another area of my life, and I had no idea how to behave towards her here. The shed in the school yard where she was stationed contained various games the pupils could borrow. A lot of them thought it fun that the shed was there, but I kept as far away as I could from it, still wondering how on earth Aunt Berit had ended up in my school.

But in the long run it was difficult to avoid her, because it turned out she was also in charge of the recreation room in the school building. One day when she saw me and stopped to chat, I asked her what she was doing there.

'I'm here to keep an eye on you.'

I suppose that was an attempt at a joke on her part, but I didn't grasp it. With my concrete way of thinking people meant precisely what they said, I thought it was true, that she had come to the school just to teach me some manners. It was a dreadful feeling. I felt persecuted and controlled. Aunt Berit's sharp, watchful and largely disapproving eyes were following me all over the school. She was going to keep an eye on me . . . it was as if she had put a curse on me.

I knew perfectly what 'keep an eye on you' meant. But nonetheless, I was uncertain whether the expression might have another meaning, something much more absolute. I saw the image of 'keeping an eye on you' very clearly, but whose eye? Was it the keeper's, or that of the person kept an eye on? As I still didn't know how other people could know about the future or about situations that they weren't present at, I thought the expression perhaps meant her eyes somehow seeing everything. Even when she wasn't present. I would spend hours and hours racking my brains and trying to work out what this all meant.

Anyway, Aunt Berit's eyes were often clearly present. If we were to have our fluoride dose, she would be there to detect any red colour that would show that I had cleaned my teeth carelessly. At weighing and measuring, Aunt Berit was there beside the school nurse with her opinions on my overweight, and her way of saying 'Ugh!' when she disapproved of something followed me all round the school.

The noise made by mopeds could be heard everywhere in the street, and I couldn't bear it. I was still very sensitive to certain sounds. It was difficult to be on my own and I was so vulnerable out of doors—it was like going around with no skin and always trying to keep everything in place nonetheless. I was raw, and if I let go for a second everything essential to life would threaten to fall out of me.

On Tuesdays and Thursdays my mother went to classes and I had to pass a white house on my way to Aunt Berit's, where I was to go on those two afternoons a week. Living in the white house, which was just beyond a crossroads, was an older girl, and she had a boy-friend, who in his turn had a moped. The girl was an empty face, but I had some vague inkling that her face ought to have some content. Perhaps she was someone's older sister? I had begun to find out that my way of seeing people was not the same as other people's. Others seemed to see chains of content in and between faces that were nothing but contours to me. They seemed to see links between parents and siblings and houses and roads that meant the people had something to do with each other. I could also occasionally link people with each other via some common denominator, but I didn't know, for instance, that it counted more to have the same mother than it did to have the same teacher.

This girl with the empty face and her boy-friend with the moped found out that I had hardly any skin on my body. They very much wanted to see if they could loosen the few small patches of skin that I still had left as protection. They did that by teasing me in a way that developed into a ritual every time I had to go to and from Aunt Berit's.

The boy and the girl used to hang around outside her house, he sitting on his moped, she leaning against the gate. When they saw that the sound of the moped made me react strangely, they started scaring me. They would wait for me to pass them, then suddenly rev the moped. The din made the ground under my feet disappear and I could neither see nor feel the world around me. Up and down were suddenly in the same place and I had no sense of where my feet were. So as not to fall over or explode from inside, I would grab the fence where I was standing, pressing myself against it and holding on hard. I had to feel something that stood still, something anchored, in a world that had suddenly become totally unpredictable. I clutched at the red-painted planks of the fence.

Perhaps it looked strange or funny, as if I was standing in a little sailing-boat in a raging storm. But I had no intellectual space left in my mind to step outside myself and see that what was happening was strange. I was so occupied trying to get a grip on the situation and to make out what was going on. When I noticed that the same thing happened every time I went to Aunt Berit's, I began to hold on to the fence when I was really quite far away— on tenterhooks as I tried to prepare myself for the hideous noise to come. Sometimes they didn't rev up, but suddenly said 'Vroom, vroom', which made me jump and them laugh. At other times they began to rev the moped the moment they saw me in the distance, so that I couldn't walk past. I simply couldn't go any closer. The noise formed a wall I couldn't get through. I stood there, a bit away from them, as long as it amused them to keep it up.

Then Aunt Berit would be cross with me for being late. She had my timetable and she certainly knew exactly how long it took to walk to her house. She knew I was lazy and cheeky. I had given up trying to tell the truth to grown-ups. There was no point. So I just stood there while she told me the reason for my lateness. I just waited until she had finished. I shut myself off and let her scolding, just like other people's, wash straight through one ear and out of the other. That made her crosser than ever, but she no longer dared to touch me.

At home, my parents' marriage was rapidly disintegrating, and they were now as good as locked in the relationship of mutual degradation. My mother increased her consumption of pills to abuse level, and both she and my father were more and more frequently drunk. As long as we all kept to ourselves, things were fairly calm in the house. But at weekends or holidays, or some other situation requiring us to be together, the mines laid earlier would be stepped on. And they exploded according to a certain pattern.

My father hit my mother. My mother hit back. My mother was beaten up.

On some occasions my father locked her in their bed-room, and it was to me that she would turn to climb up the fire ladder and hand her the key through the upper balcony window. She was far too unsteady to get out that way, though, and I was simply not allowed to unlock the door from the outside, for then she would be beaten up again. I was to filch the key from my father, or find an extra one—some of the inside doors had the same key, and it took some time for my father to grasp that he had to collect up all of them in order to stop my mother getting out. Then I was to slip outside and climb up to the first floor—which in fact was the second floor on that side of the house because the basement there was above ground. I would climb the fire escape, a ladder up the side of the house; then I'd take a few steps on to the downpipe, heave myself over the edge of the balcony and give the key to my mother. She usually sent me back down the same way because she didn't want to go out at once—she just wanted to know that she could get out if she needed to. I did as I was told. She would call out to me through the door what I was to do, and I didn't think about it, just did as she said.

I didn't give much thought, either, to whether I ought or ought not to obey her orders. I couldn't do what Kerstin did—weigh up whether she felt so sorry for my mother that she should help her, or whether she would tell her that it was their business, not hers. Kerstin was full of rules for whether they could demand things of her or not, and she was also full of emotions which fought against her rules. I just did things. And whatever I did, in Kerstin's eyes, it was always the wrong thing. But anyway, I did overcome my vertigo in this way. After climbing the fire escape, I was also able to climb up the wall bars in the gym. What I learnt, I had to learn for myself, from necessity and compulsion. From my mother's drinking and my father's violence.

Otherwise, it was mostly my sister who became, or demonstratively refused to become, involved in their quarrels. I was just there as a kind of absent presence, trying to be left alone. But if they asked me something I could understand and could carry out, I did as they asked without thinking about whether it was right or wrong. I never understood why my sister took a stand, or what lay behind her involvement. The older I grew, the more clearly I saw how it disturbed Kerstin that I didn't care much about what my mother and father got up to. To her it was important and she was careful to try to keep up appearances. On the other hand, I had no sense whatsoever of what should be seen on the outside or of what shouldn't be talked about. I felt no need to keep my parents' misery from view. If they didn't ensure that I washed, had socks on my feet and clean clothes, I didn't do it myself instead. I just wore rubber boots, with no socks, my clothes stayed dirty and I didn't clean my teeth. While Kerstin washed the family's façade, I neither washed nor polished. This annoyed her. She was torn between bothering about me—wanting to make sure I was properly dressed, whole and clean—and wanting to lock me up somewhere so that I shouldn't bring shame on her carefully scrubbed surface.

I had now acquired the right clothes—the same kinds as the others wore at school—but what use was this when I still spilt things on them? I lost buttons. My shirt was always half tucked in, half hanging out. I simply couldn't look 'right', because I had no natural feeling for it. I was always quite unaware I was sloppily dressed until someone pointed out the stains or something else that was wrong, and then I was ashamed. I was acutely aware that I was in the wrong, but I didn't know how to do anything about it. Why couldn't they just leave me alone?

My very presence seemed to trigger things in people. It was as if I released in them harsh maternal instincts and a desire to tidy me up. Or else I seemed to provoke them just by existing. People would lick their fingers and wipe some stain or other off my face, tug at my clothes and try to smooth down my hair. I couldn't understand why they thought they had the right to mess me about at all, but I learnt just to stand still and endure it until they had stopped messing and left me alone.

I didn't know why they did it. No person or thing ever aroused any desire in me to intervene and change things. Nothing had ever annoyed me as much as it seemed to annoy them. I felt neither the desire nor any need to change things or interfere in what the world got up to, so it was incomprehensible that the world simply wouldn't leave me to my own devices. How could I guess that they had quite different inner driving forces from mine, and that they thought people really were concerned about each other?

People messing me about was accompanied by a sort of chant that followed me all through my childhood.

Pick up your feet! Look what you're doing! Sit up!
Chew your food,
eat properly,
sit up properly. Look where you're going.
You *must* learn
to pick up your feet,
chew your food,
look where you're going.
Sit up. Listen properly. Don't try to get out of it.
Pull yourself together.
Sit down there now,
eat this now,
do as I say.
Don't sit like a sack of potatoes,
don't stamp about like that,
pick your feet up, I said.
For the thousandth time, chew your food properly.

Eat with your mouth shut.
Be quiet.
Pick up your feet.
How many times do I have to tell you?
Don't make faces. Take your fingers out of your mouth.
Sit up straight. Don't drag your feet like that.
Answer when you're spoken to.
Stop grinning.
Look at me. Listen when I speak to you.
Listen to what I say.
Don't be so lazy. Don't be cheeky.
Don't be.
Pull yourself together and stop doing that.
Make an effort now.
You can if you want to.
Listen to what I say.
Look where you're going. Don't drop that now.
Pick up your feet, I said.

My inner refrain went: 'No real person—no real person—
no real person'.

I never understood that 'Pick up your feet.' I was flat-
footed and walked on my whole foot, with my toes turned
slightly inwards. I had never learnt to walk in that involved
way that meant angling my foot up and putting my heel
down first, a prerequisite for being able to *pick up your
feet*. I wore my shoes down in no time at all, because I
dragged my feet along the ground when walking. But
when they told me to pick up my feet, to me that meant
lifting my whole foot right up and with it my leg, then
parading along with my knees raised high. It was horribly
hard work and I could never work out whether that was
really what they wanted me to do. So I went on dragging
my feet along the ground. I also refused to throw away
my down-at-heel shoes, and used to wear wooden-soled
ones that were too small for me, the soles worn right down

to a slippery, thin, inward-sloping sliver. I had no proper arches, and new shoes were uncomfortable however right for my feet they were considered to be. There were several reasons why I wanted to keep my worn and much-too-small old shoes. It was because everything else hurt my feet, but also because in general I didn't like new things. I just liked things that were familiar, things I was used to, so they couldn't cause me any surprises. There were battles over what I was to wear on my feet. I usually won.

The fact that I interpreted what people said to me so concretely did create some problems. My mother might come into my room before going off to her English class and say 'Can you empty the dishwasher?'

'Yes,' I would reply.

Two hours later, when she was scolding me for not having done what I'd promised to do, I could only be amazed.

'What?'

I hadn't understood that she had meant me to *do* it. I had just answered in quite absolute terms. 'Can you . . . ?'—'Yes, I can.' In the same way as if she had said 'Can you speak English?' But my parents could see no reason for my behaviour except that I was ill-mannered, nasty and lazy. All scolding, all complaints, all nagging, all those 'You ought to', 'You must' and 'Can't you ever learn?' ended up depositing humiliation inside me. By the time I was about three, it all began to settle in a thin layer under my skin, at about ankle height. Then new layers built up, layer after layer of the fact that I ought to be someone else inside. It grew to knee height. New layers, up to my shoulders and neck, of 'I'm not a real person . . . Not a real person, never ever a real person' filled me entirely—in the end right out to the roots of my hair.

My dislike of surprises applied to all areas of life. I didn't want to be surprised, not ever. If I was to have any chance of coping with situations, I had to be prepared for them. I might like to be given presents, but I found it hard work not knowing what they contained. As jewellery was so terrifying to touch, I preferred to be prepared for the contents of all presents—just in case. My absolutely favourite present was the one I had every Christmas and which I could quite easily recognise from the outside. I could recognise that parcel under the Christmas tree from a long way away. You couldn't mistake the shape. It contained a large tin of pineapple, which was one of my fixations—and so every year I was given a whole tin which was mine and mine alone.

I was so secure in this Christmas present ritual that I even tolerated having jokes made about it, something I otherwise found difficult to endure. One Christmas, the tin of pineapple had been exchanged for a roll of lavatory paper. I was terribly surprised when I opened the parcel, but I realised at once that it was a joke and the real tin was somewhere around. It was a powerful and amazing experience, the feeling of actually being amused at them playing a joke on me.

Christmas and its demands for family togetherness always provoked quarrels, and a lot of Christmas trees ended up on the floor. But despite everything, what my parents got up to didn't bother me all that much. To me, the tin of pineapple under the tree was the most important thing of all. But this didn't mean that I didn't notice their fights. I saw everything.

1973 Evening—mother knocks the tree down—Crash!
1975 Morning—mother has already knocked the tree down—Crash!
1976 Father shoves mother into the tree—Crash!

My mother and father would appear to be performing

an incomprehensible dance around the tree, my father's hands now and again around her throat, or his fist in her eye. But my mother wasn't just being led in this dance, although she might offer a semblance of the weak and manipulated wife. She could also suddenly execute an unexpected solo number in this destructive performance. When you thought she had been knocked out and counted down long ago, she would rise with tomahawk aloft and dance her own war dance. She wasn't *just* a victim—she liked to fight back, though there was never any doubt who was the stronger.

I watched all this. I saw it. But I couldn't understand what it really meant, or what attitude I should take towards it. So I didn't do anything, I ignored it. Kerstin talked agitatedly to me, her cheeks flushed and her head moving oddly on her neck. I didn't understand the emotion that made her look like that, but I did recognise that drab but slightly glossy wine-red colour in her which I understood a little better—despair. I was sorry for her when she was that wine-red colour and her head wobbled like that. It somehow seemed so unnecessary.

One day Kerstin said that our parents would probably separate. 'Oh yes.' I didn't know what that meant. She tried to explain, but I couldn't relate it in any way to me. I heard what she said, but didn't think it seemed all that terrible. I couldn't see it in front of me. Separate. Live in different places. It just ran through my mind without finding anywhere to lodge.

Eleven

I was very lonely, and was increasingly suffering from it—
not from my actual solitude, but more from comparing
myself with others and wanting to be as normal, right and
ordinary as they were. My actual solitude—being on my
own—was easy. I found it much easier to be on my own
than to be with other people. I never missed other people
when I was drawing, reading or writing poems, or when
I was examining and investigating things. I never felt I
ought to have wanted to share them with anyone; in fact,
the thought never even entered my head. Yet that emptiness was my eternal companion, like a vague loss of something; though at the same time I was so used to it, I
couldn't imagine things could be any other way.

At school, I maintained my odd position. I was wrong
in every conceivable way. I was silent and peculiar, and I
accepted withering words and blows. At the same time, I
had this incredible integrity and fearlessness that gave me
the courage to punch the nastiest and strongest bully in
the school, to bite any teacher who tried to get hold of
me, and to bring cigarettes to school in order to try smoking them without caring whether anyone saw me. Though
none of this was a question of courage or toughness—it
was simply that I couldn't really see the consequences of
certain actions, and also that physical pain meant nothing
special to me.

Some in my class did try approaching me. The children
who bullied me were mostly from other classes, but I
didn't really know that, as I had such a poor sense of who
was who. Now, with new insights into my failings, I was

suspicious of everyone. I never knew what their intentions were and didn't comprehend their way of trying to make contact with me. If I didn't want to be deceived, it was safest to keep away from them all.

By now I could sometimes recognise some of my class-mates outside the classroom. But I still often had only a vague feeling that I ought to know that person, without really being able to put my finger on who it was. This was a step forward, of course—when I'd been at junior school I hadn't the slightest idea who I was expected to recognise. But I'd felt safer then, and now I was less certain and had some inkling that perhaps I ought to know more. So this increased my suspiciousness.

I tried to keep up with my school work, and the fact that I was so incredibly good at some things meant that they expected me to be just as good in other fields. It wasn't so. The moment mathematics involved more than just the four ways of calculating, one after another, I lost all grasp of it. Incomprehensible new symbols were now to represent various things—$< \geq \approx \neq \%$—and I couldn't get them to stay in my head however hard I tried. I couldn't open the hatch to the compartment they were supposed to be in. The symbols slid around and got lost in my mind. If I tried to slip in the meaning of a new one, inevitably another fell out. There was simply no room.

Furthermore, maths involved thinking along several lines that I couldn't manage. I always had to think one thing at a time, because I couldn't find any place in my mind in which to put a thought aside. I had to hold on to the thought, actively hold on to it as if with an inner 'hand', while I reallocated a little energy in order to be able to concentrate on something else at the same time. This required immense concentration. If I managed to remain undisturbed, I could manually balance one thought on each 'finger' while I went on examining another, but then I had to work out clues to find my way back to them in the right order. Someone near by only had to cough for me to lose part of the thought. And if I lost a part of it, everything collapsed and I had to start all over again from the beginning. But as I didn't know what other people could do, or how they did things, I thought it was my laziness that prevented me from finding the energy. If I could grasp a symbol via my feeling for poetry, I might learn it, but to me mathematical symbols were totally without poetry, as were chemical formulae. Nor did musical notes seem able to engage my feeling for poetry. I didn't understand them at all.

As I couldn't play any instrument, music was another of the school subjects I was bad at. I liked singing to myself, but I knew nothing about notes and couldn't hear the difference between them, so perhaps my singing those long incantations of words I had invented had only been a way of keeping my nervous system going. But my mother thought singing might be an interest, and she very much wanted me to have interests. Kerstin was in the Guides, Kerstin danced, Kerstin had friends, and my mother wanted to activate me. She got it into her head that I could be in the school choir, and she succeeded in persuading me to want to join it. But by the time I had got as far as allowing myself to be persuaded, it turned out that you had to be auditioned.

I joined the queue of children outside the music room. We were to go in one by one and sing a song. The music teacher was at the piano, her face powdered white, her hair black, bright-red patches on her cheeks. I had never seen a white-faced woman with black hair before, and I'd never sung alone to a piano before, either. After I had sung the song we had to sing, 'Little Snail Beware', the teacher said I'd sung some wrong notes. I knew nothing about notes. She tried to show me on the piano, but I was none the wiser. Then she said it was all right, anyway, and

I was to go out and tell the next person to come in, the one with a surname beginning with H.

I thought I was going to be allowed to join the choir. She had said it was all right. If she'd said I'd sung badly I would have understood that I wouldn't be allowed to join. But I didn't find out until afterwards, from my mother, that I couldn't. I was unhappy that it was all so strange and contradictory, that I had been persuaded to want to do something that I then wasn't allowed to. And why had she said it was all right?

The same music mistress silenced me completely a few years later. When the girls in my class were to be the attendants in the Lucia procession, she took me to one side and said it would be best if I mimed to the singing, as I sang so badly. That silenced me. I stopped singing completely, and for ever, and I wondered why no one had told me before. I wondered whether out of some sort of misdirected kindness people didn't want to tell me what was wrong with me. I wondered again whether I was perhaps backward, as I myself hadn't understood that I should keep quiet, hadn't even grasped that I sounded so peculiar.

On the other hand, I did notice I occasionally failed to take things in, like when my mother and Kerstin wanted to teach me how to use the washing-machine. They explained, and I looked on. They explained several times. But then when I was to do it on my own, I couldn't work it. The switches on the machine were so alike and I couldn't remember what they were for. They thought they had shown me so many times, many more times than I ought to need—in fact, more times than *anyone* ought to need. And with their monopoly of the truth, they confirmed that it was out of idleness that I couldn't be bothered to learn to use the machine and, of course, I just wanted to be waited on.

They didn't know how long I had stood on my own in

front of the washing-machine trying to work out what to do. I couldn't remember what they had said and didn't dare risk pressing the wrong switch, as I didn't know what might happen if I did.

Maybe I would have managed if they had first outlined verbally how a washing-machine works, and what happens inside it. And if they'd then given me written instructions and let me press the right switches, preferably several times, I could have put the memory into my fingertips.

I now looked inside myself for some explanation of why I couldn't work the washing-machine. There was nothing there, no explanation hanging on any hook. Even the hooks seemed to have been unscrewed. So it had to be because I was lazy, although I didn't know it myself. Their image of the world was unhesitating and crystal-clear. After so many explanations you can carry out a given task, and if you know one thing it means you automatically know another. They had looked for, and found, the patent for the way things worked. Faced with their massive superiority, how could I even begin to imagine they might be wrong?

I didn't want to have to endure any more surprises, so when I was twelve I resolved to expose myself to everything quite voluntarily until nothing was left undone, nothing could surprise me. I would lay myself open to absolutely everything—everything imaginable. I would be part of everything once, and so be ready for everything. Intuitively, I had realised experience was necessary to my nervous system. I saw that as I was unable to transfer knowledge automatically from one area to another, I had to have experience of every conceivable situation in order to be able to prepare for it. In time I almost forgot my resolution, but subconsciously I stuck to it. Over the years I was to have a great many unpleasant and destructive experiences. The resolution almost kept itself—all I had to do was go with it as it rolled along. The more I saw, the more I wearied of living, and in this way I laid myself open to more and more destructive things.

The summer before I was to go to senior high school, my parents had been working hard at the final stages of demolishing what had previously been at least something resembling a family. The borderline between who was adult and who was child, a borderline that had always been rather blurred in our family, became almost invisible. My mother and father hit each other. My father also hit Kerstin, and my mother didn't dare intervene. She preferred her elder daughter to take the punishment rather than receive the blows herself. It pained me to see Kerstin being hit so many times. I thought it would have been better if he had lashed out at me instead, as I was not as sensitive as she was. But he hardly ever hit me—it didn't have much effect. Kerstin, on the other hand, was subdued, in despair, and she also felt the physical pain.

It was good to be left to my own devices, although I also suffered from the effects of the general family chaos. I no longer wanted to be at home; things were far too difficult. So I started staying out late in the evenings. No other children were out as late as I was in this middle-class residential area. I was out there in my solitude. The world was quieter then, and it looked just as deserted as it felt. That tallied. I swung on the swings in empty parks and walked the streets on my own, observing the deserted scene. I liked it when things tallied, when there was both an internal and an external emptiness.

Down by our commuter railway station I could see people, and teenagers hung around there with cans of beer, but it never occurred to me to join them. I just wanted to be on my own. It was difficult not being able to be at home, not having any refuge to be alone in, for out of doors was not really safe. It could be cold and I hadn't always enough clothes on. People felt free to come up to me and ask what I was doing out at that time, and this was always problematical. I didn't know what to say, so I didn't answer.

My mother sometimes lost all sense of how old I was. One moment I would be given presents I was much too old for, and the next she would be giving me detailed information on sexual matters for which I was far too young. But she mostly slept, or lay dozing somewhere. Now and again, she woke up so that she and my father could start screaming at each other, swearing and hitting each other.

Sometimes they went out together. They went to parties, and when they came home they would both be so drunk that they couldn't get up the stairs to their bedroom. Or my mother would be sent home in a taxi, swearing and shouting, or in a near-psychotic state, while my father went on enjoying himself at the party.

Kerstin tried to involve me in rescue operations, but I would retreat into myself, or out on to the streets. I kept thinking—I was trying to understand all the things I didn't understand. I wondered about why people mispronounced words and didn't speak them as they were spelt. If it was spelt like that, then it should be spoken like that, shouldn't it? And yet people said words both ways. I tried to detect some system within words themselves that would tell me when it should be one way or the other.

I pondered on why it said 'by popular request' when they sometimes repeated things in comics. How could they know they were popular? Did they have secret polls? Did children write in to the comics to tell them what they thought? The idea that it might just be someone inventing what was to be popular never even occurred to me.

I often went around thinking about things I had read but wasn't sure I had understood. It was very difficult when the sides of the boxes in the comics were of different lengths, and I was never sure what order I should read them in. I wanted there to be an absolutely definite sequence of boxes, so that I would be able to work out what I was missing when I wasn't sure about the order of events in the story. I wondered if different-sized boxes with no arrows between them meant that they could be read in various ways, in any order you liked. I thought that seemed reasonable, as sometimes there *were* arrows in between which showed in which order the strip should be read—though it had to be difficult to think up a plot that could be read in several different ways ... I never really managed to fathom how it worked. I always felt that there must be one general rule governing the various bits and that all you had to do was to work it out.

In the summer between the sixth and seventh grades I had my first period. It was in 1976, and the last summer we spent in Åland. By then I wasn't the only one to be uncommunicative. My mother slept all the time, my father was absorbed in his own rage, and Kerstin was keeping a diary. So I was left in peace. But then that blood was there. I saw it one day when I was in the outside privy and something had to be done about it. I was troubled, not by the period itself, but because I would now have to make contact with them. I didn't want to be a child any longer and dependent on them. I didn't want to have anything to do with them.

I told Kerstin about it, hoping that would be enough. But my mother, suddenly emerging from her unconscious state, thought it fun that her younger daughter had grown up and become a woman. I hadn't wanted to tell her at all, but Kerstin had told me that I had to so that she could sort out whatever I needed for protection. We were out in the country and there was no shop we could go to. My mother gave me a packet of Tampax Super Plus with an insertion tube.

I sat in the privy staring at these huge tube-like objects.

146

I didn't know what to do with them. Nor did I realise how undiscerning it had been of her—a woman with heavy periods, who had given birth to two children—to give me these things of hers. And I simply couldn't bring myself to try putting one in. I threw the packet away and put toilet paper in my pants instead.

After that, I continued to use toilet paper. There were quite long gaps between my periods and not all that much blood. I said nothing more about it to my mother or to Kerstin. Long afterwards, Kerstin discovered I was still using toilet paper, and she got hold of money from mother to buy something of a suitable size.

Now I was to start at senior school. Just when I had at last learnt to find my way around my old school, and just when I had begun to recognise the people there, I was flung into a new school—a comprehensive containing an endless number of empty faces, more than I had ever been afflicted with before, more than I could imagine existed— perhaps eight hundred pupils in all. There were endless corridors, classrooms and other buildings, and row upon row of identical lockers everywhere.

The empty faces seethed all around me. I tried to cope with this during my first term. I made a real effort, but striving to concentrate on school work became too much when all my energy went on calculating how to deal with everything around me. How would I find the right class-room? Where was the dining-room? Which book did I need for the next lesson? Which was my locker? Who was that suddenly walking past and saying hullo? Was it someone I knew? What did those symbols telling me what the next lesson was mean?

I tried to solve the problems in a creative way. I reckoned that I could be off sick when we were to have a test, because then I would have to do it later, on my own. And sitting alone in a cubby-hole meant that I had much better conditions in which to do the test than if I was in class with all those little sounds and movements distracting me. But this worked only until some teacher thought it suspicious that I was always ill when there was a test. They thought perhaps I was cheating. But I wasn't. That would have been totally against my sense of the rules; also, I had no particular feeling that marks were important. Anyway, I wasn't allowed to do the tests alone any longer, and I was put in with another class if I had to do one later. This made it even worse for me. Then I had to find my way to another classroom and sit in a room full of vacant faces. So there was no point in being ill for tests.

When I had to find my way to the various classrooms in school, I usually tried to tag along with the others in my class. This meant that I couldn't go to the lavatory in the short breaks, as then I risked losing sight of them. And if I couldn't go with them, I often lost my way and that was painful. I didn't want to have to ask. I didn't like talking to those vacant faces, but I was sometimes forced to ask someone. I tried to persuade myself that they perhaps thought I was just visiting the school, so needed to ask the way. Though that didn't work very well. I had begun to think that perhaps my face was not as empty to others as theirs were to me. I felt they thought it strange that I couldn't find my way. It was often no use asking, because they might reply 'This or that corridor on the left, number this or that on the door'. This was no use. I didn't really know left from right, and all the corridors were so alike that they merged together, sliding into each other. Nor was there enough difference between the little numbers on the right of the doors.

All this was also made more difficult by the constant murmur created by hundreds of pupils in an old stone building with high ceilings. This murmur was torment to me, as if eating into my mind, as if penetrating between my thoughts and making them dusty and hairy. My thoughts grew ragged at the edges, and I couldn't dismiss the sound if it lasted too long. Trying to block it out was usually too much of an effort. All that was left to me was to let go and switch off the whole system. To retreat inside myself.

I still didn't know how the lavatory business worked. I hadn't worked out how to tell the difference between them, and in several places in this school the lavatories were either single or three in a row. My idea of gents and ladies applied only if there were two alongside each other, and I could easily go to those lavatories without thinking about it. Anyway, this school was so disorientating and confusing, with all those pupils, that no one noticed if you went to a lavatory in another part of it.

In my second term I no longer made a special effort in any area, and I increasingly disappeared into myself. In many ways, I became as I had been when I was three years old, before my temper tantrums began, as if I had a kind of inner fuse which simply switched off the current when I was overloaded.

Screening off like this was provocative to those around me—they seemed to regard my total indifference as a personal affront, as if directed at them in particular. I simply couldn't understand why I had that effect on people—why the less *I* reacted, the more they did. According to my logic, they ought to leave me alone, just as I left them alone. My very uneven achievements in school also seemed to provoke them. Without any effort, I got top marks in Swedish, English, French and Art. I often had to correct my teachers of Swedish because I knew all the alternative spellings a word could have, and I always adhered to the original spelling, which I considered the most correct.

I had an almost photographic memory for a certain type of text, and this was useful when it came to languages. Texts that were either in alphabetical order or divided into numbered paragraphs, as they are in a grammar book, easily stuck in my mind. I had read the whole of the English grammar book and could leaf through to a page in my head for any paragraph I needed. In some ways, I didn't really remember what was there, but I had a kind of copy of the page in my head, which I was then able to read off.

Of course, this talent had its uses in my later studies. But unfortunately, what stuck in my head—words from dictionaries in alphabetical order, paragraphs in civil service regulations, the nutritional content of foodstuffs in National Food Administration tables—was often of the kind that you didn't really need to know, but could just as well look up when you needed to. I was a maverick in the educational reforms of the Seventies, in which everything was to be simplified, made more accessible to the masses.

My teacher of Swedish also took history and geography, as well as being our class teacher. It seemed to annoy him immensely that in Swedish lessons I was able to write good essays, give the right answers in all the tests and apparently be involved in what I was doing, but then in the next lesson, geography, I might be completely absent, not answering when spoken to and getting few of the answers correct in tests. In his eyes, the fault could only be mine. He often made me stay behind after lessons to try to make me see sense.

'Gunilla, stay behind, will you? You others can go.'

'You can all go five minutes earlier today. Gunilla—you stay behind.'

'You can go home now, all except Gunilla. I want to speak to her.'

I stayed behind, but I wasn't there. It was as if he was talking to an empty body. He tried various ways—shouting at me, admonishing me, appealing to me, cajoling me. Nothing got through. I knew what was going on around me, but it had nothing to do with me. In a way, I heard what he was saying, but it seemed to stop at the outer edges of my ears; it had no particular significance. To him, it was the height of insolence that I could be so unmoved. But I was in no way being insolent, only wanting to be left alone, feeling a very intense desire to be left in peace.

In the eighth grade, I started taking a different attitude to school. I became tougher and developed a little of what was indeed insolence, pure insolence. The fact that I chose this strategy, the cold, tough approach, was due to the misery at home—no one cared for me so why should I care about anything?—and to the fact that the school had already decided that this was what I was like, anyway. Look after yourself and to hell with anyone else, better to forestall than be forestalled, became my policy. When we had tests in subjects of which I understood nothing, like maths, chemistry or physics, I would just nonchalantly take the test paper, write my name on it and hand it in without looking at it. This was essentially logical. Why should I humiliate myself by sitting for three-quarters of an hour staring at a paper that demanded something of me that I had no hope of coping with? My behaviour drove the teachers demented, especially as I went on getting high marks in some subjects. But gradually my inaccessibility had the desired effect. Most of the teachers gave up and left me alone.

Twelve

My father had moved out, the last word spoken. My parents were now to separate, but that meant nothing to me until I realised that we were to move house. My sister had dragged my mother round to look at various apartments and now they had decided on one. I had heard them talking about it, but I hadn't thought it had anything to do with me. As I hadn't twigged that we were to move, I hadn't bothered about what they were up to. Then suddenly I understood what was to happen. I didn't want to move house, most certainly not. Our house and garden were my security. The house was closer to me than people were. But I had no say in it all.

My mother had started drinking more and more frequently. When she had been drinking *and* taking pills, she went into at the very least a pre-psychotic state, rambling on, talking in brutally coarse sexual terms, hallucinating.

My father had already moved in with another woman. He had exchanged us for other things, for a new family to possess. Now he also wanted a house to put his new woman into. His parents had recently died, fairly soon after each other, and their house was empty. It was in an increasingly popular area, and its value was going up. He wanted that house, but first of all he had to buy out the other heirs. All those with a right to the inheritance, including my mother, were now to get together and settle the sale. They were to meet at our house because my mother was not in a fit state to be taken anywhere.

When the relatives arrived, my mother had locked

herself in her room and was in bed with a large bottle of vodka. The relatives took tea in the living-room, and waited. My father told me to go up and tell my mother to come down—the kind of order I obeyed but that Kerstin would have refused. She would have refused to go and fetch mother because she thought they should do that kind of thing themselves, not involve us children in their problems. So she was often angry with me when I acted as a kind of intermediary. But I had no means of seeing those aspects of the matter. I couldn't analyse the situation and choose one behaviour one time and different behaviour the next. I just did as I was told. I was asked, or ordered, to do a simple and easily grasped thing, so I did it.

I went up, knocked on the door and told my mother she was to come out, to come down, that they were waiting downstairs. In reply, she blurted out a few slurred oaths.

'They can go to hell.'

'You must come now, Mother,' I said.

'You fucking well can't tell me what to do.'

'But they're waiting . . .'

'Go to hell.'

'But Father said that . . .'

'He can go to hell too.'

'But . . .'

'Scram! Go to hell.'

I went back down to the relations. They were still having tea, still waiting. They rattled their cups, tinkle tinkle, above the silence. No one said anything. Suddenly my mother was heard coming down the stairs, giggling and singing. She came into the room where Kerstin, father, my aunts and uncles and I were sitting. She was stark-naked, pallid and white, covered with bruises. Only the whites of her eyes were visible. She had no eyes in her eyes, only whiteness, eyelashes fluttering. She held on to the bookcase, all the time about to slide down to the floor as if she had soap under her feet. She said something no one could hear and then collapsed into a pallid, naked heap on the floor.

I thought it disgusting, distasteful, and I had no idea what had happened. I just stared. Kerstin's cheeks went all blotchy red. She dragged mother back up to her room, then shut herself into her own. I felt nothing special at the sight of my mother, but my sister's despair did move me. I didn't want her to be distraught like that. I had no idea what I should do about it. I didn't know what it was all about, but I didn't want her to be miserable.

Eventually my father and my troubled aunts and uncles went home and left the two of us, thirteen and sixteen years old, to look after this maltreated and mentally broken person who was supposed to be our mother.

'You're strong,' said one of the aunts, patting me on the head before she left.

I couldn't think what she meant and was disturbed by what had happened. I wanted a quiet, calm, secluded world. I was also very unhappy because Kerstin was always so disappointed in me. I always did the wrong thing, always too much or too little. I could sense that she had wanted to have a better younger sister than I was.

Kerstin tried involving me in everything that was going on, but inside me there was no involvement. I began to perceive that I was probably unnaturally horrible in some way, as I wasn't upset or wretched about my mother's alcoholism. I didn't bother about her, so somehow it must be my fault. *Was* it my fault, perhaps, that she was like this? She had always said so, that I drove her mad. And now she *was* mad. That was just what she was—mad, insane—and I had driven her to it.

One evening just before we were to move, mother was going to a neighbour's for dinner. I was at home watching television. I thought she had already gone, but then the telephone rang and it was the neighbour wondering

154

where my mother had got to. I told her mother had already left, but the neighbour asked me to see if she was still in the house. She would hold on. I put the receiver to one side and opened the door into the hall. I was going to go upstairs to see whether she was in her room, but I could only open the door a little way. It hit something hard. Clonk, clonk, clonk it went when I pushed harder to get whatever it was in the way to move. But whatever was there wouldn't budge, nor could I open the door wide enough to see what it was. After a while I let go of the door and went round the other way via the kitchen and dining-room into the hall. Mother was lying on the floor; it was her head I had been hitting with the door. Clonk.

She didn't really look like herself, so I wasn't totally sure it was her. She was glistening and pallid, as if made of marble. She was lying very neatly, flat out on her back with her arms folded across her chest, as if bound like a mummy. Her face looked ghastly. I poked her, but she didn't move. She looked dead, quite definitely dead. I went back to the phone and told the neighbour that my mother was lying on the hall floor. She asked what the matter was and I said I didn't know. After a while, she came round to the house, phoned for an ambulance, then left. I sat on the stairs looking out of the window as I waited for the ambulance. Everything seemed very unreal. Mother was lying without moving on the floor below me. I didn't want to touch her any more because she looked so dreadful. In the end, the ambulance came with two men, and they asked me things.

'What has she taken?'

I said I didn't know. They shone a torch into her eyes and talked to her. She mumbled something.

'Stomach pump,' they decided, and took her away with them.

Before they left, they asked whether any adult would

be coming home soon, and I heard in their voices that they wanted me to say yes, so I did. 'Yes.'

Then they said my mother would soon be back home again, after she had had her stomach pumped. I didn't know what that was, or when 'soon' might be. But I didn't particularly want her to come back. I thought it was a good idea that they were taking that repulsive, horrible thing away with them. I didn't know how I could even begin to understand all this. I went back and watched television while I waited for the possibility of my sister coming home.

The actual move took place a few weeks later. My mother had locked herself and her cheap vodka into her bedroom. Some months earlier, soon after my father had moved out, she had begun locking herself in there. One day she staggered out and collected up all the keys of the house. Dirty and evil-smelling, she had pulled herself together and demanded that all of the keys be handed over to her. She wanted to devote herself to her drinking undisturbed. When Kerstin tried involving me in pouring away her spirits, and in other anxious attempts to stop her drinking, I didn't understand why she wanted me to. I didn't want to go anywhere near this person. I couldn't make out the point of worrying. I just wanted to be left alone.

Kerstin took on the move. I couldn't fathom what she was doing, and kept out of the way as best I could. The contents of a large house had to be cleared and packed, then squeezed into a four-room apartment. That was a lot of work for a sixteen-year-old to manage alone. She tried insisting that I help, and I did my best to wriggle out of it. I didn't know what moving house entailed, I'd never done it before. I couldn't imagine living anywhere else and so everything that was happening was incomprehensible. I kept out of the way, either physically or mentally— usually both.

I became more and more detached. I had found a kind of higher level of detachment than I had had before. When I was younger, I had usually gone into that state just occasionally, and I used to look passive, then, even if I was doing something. Now I was able to live the whole day—get up and go to school, eat and watch television—all in a state of detachment. I mostly didn't hear when people spoke to me. I could stare right through them. I felt as if I was almost transparent, as if I could let people who wanted something pass through me in a way, and out the other side, without them leaving the slightest trace in me—as if I was made of an entirely different substance. Nor could I grasp, intellectually, that it had anything to do with me whatsoever.

I had no inkling of the effect I had on other people, that they were provoked by my unmoved exterior. I was slapped and shaken and pushed by both my sister and the teachers, but I no longer felt any pain at all. In fact, my insensitivity to pain was by now as good as total. Until then I had just been insensitive to certain pains, but now nothing hurt at all. And yet I felt—my actual feelings were not shut off—because when I was aware that I had injured myself somewhere, I could sense something, a non-pain, which branched out into my body from the place where the injury was. But the fact was, it didn't hurt.

On the other hand, one thing that was still very difficult to endure was light touches, the kind that went no more than skin-deep. Everything else I hardly registered at all. So I liked going to the school dentist, now in the same building as the school, the same dentists I hadn't been able to find when I was younger. I just sat there and let them get on with it. I found it pleasant, with no one requiring me to talk or do anything. At the same time I felt I was being cared for in a way that did not breach my integrity threshold.

Because my motor system was so clumsy, I was always

falling over and hitting myself, or twisting or spraining an ankle. So it was no surprise that I fell over and knocked out a tooth when I was thirteen. Perhaps my feeling of safety with the dentist had something to do with it, subconsciously. I often had to go to the dentist, and also to a special children's dental clinic in town. This was even better, because I would miss several lessons on account of the travelling. Missing school was a relief. Every moment I didn't have to be there was a gain, although I never played truant because my sense that rules were there to be obeyed prevented it from entering my head. Perhaps I would have puzzled my teachers less if I *had* played truant. It seemed to annoy them hugely when I displayed a toughness and a lack of concern that exceeded even that of the roughest boys—handing in blank test papers and not doing my homework, maintaining the long, unbroken silences during lessons; but at the same time obeying all the rules, never trying to impress people, achieving top marks in several subjects, and, whenever I did open my mouth, speaking well and precisely. I realised I was bewildering and peculiar in some way. But why everyone appeared to regard me as a personal defeat, I simply could not fathom.

As often as I could, I tried to arrange these dental visits so that they would fall during maths lessons. Now in senior school, I could make no headway at all with maths, and knew only the four ways of calculating, nothing more. However many explanations I was given, it made no difference, and if I grasped something for a while, it was never in my head for long. I never understood it from inside, but just learnt to carry out certain superficial procedures—add this first, then subtract that—without the slightest idea of why I was doing it.

My maths teacher was a large man with a deep, harsh voice, and he liked scaring his pupils. When he wasn't frightening them by using this voice, he often stood at the front of the classroom trying to catch with his tongue the cord hanging from the white screen in the ceiling. Now and again, he would turn round and draw or write something on the blackboard. I couldn't make out what it was he was writing, but occasionally I did actually get some things right in maths tests. In a back-to-front way and with my own logic I had reached the right answer, but I had no hope of accounting on paper for how I had done it. So I got no marks however right the answer was, because it didn't count if you couldn't say how and why. Just knowing was useless. I gradually stopped trying to work things out, as it seemed so meaningless. So I was now also handing in blank maths test papers. At first I carefully wrote my name and class on the dotted lines, and if nothing was said I was then able to put the paper on the teacher's desk in front of him and leave the room. But sometimes he made it quite clear that I had to stay there for a while before I could go. Then I would look out of the window until the time came and I could hand in the test paper. I actually didn't know that this was such provocative behaviour. I didn't think my actions affected others in this way. Of course, I knew the point was that pupils were to do the test, but as I simply couldn't . . . After all, they were my marks and it was my life.

The maths master tried using his terror tactics on me, crashing the pointer down on my desk right in front of me. CRASH! He cracked it down like a whip. The usual effect of this was that the pupils were scared, and jumped. He didn't scare me. The pointer came whistling down and struck the open book in front of me, and I scarcely blinked. I was inside myself, and my nervous system was not switched on enough to react to what he had done. I merely noted it. Ah yes . . . And as I'd seen him doing the same thing to others, it did not surprise me.

Nevertheless, there was something remarkable, both sad and amusing, about this maths teacher—I sensed he had some respect for me, that he respected me in a very special way, as if he was the only one to understand my need to maintain my integrity. He was the only one who never tried to step in with smarmy words about what I ought to do or how I should be. He tried his methodology, but when it didn't succeed he left me alone, accepting that in me he had met his match.

Now that we had moved, I had to start going to school by bus. Although I didn't at all like the apartment we had moved into, I thought it marked my outsiderness very well. Now I no longer lived in the elitist middle-class area where the school was, and I had to take the bus from a suburb of apartment blocks. Also, I chose more consciously to distance myself from the crowd. I did still want to be a real person, but not like the others at school. I wore a Palestinian scarf, Lapp boots, corduroys and a duffel coat when everyone else wore lace blouses and loafers. Or else I wore men's clothes, real old-men's clothes, which I liked. This was not intended as a direct provocation on my part, but that was how it looked, and I thought it just as well that my non-belonging was visible on the outside.

When fashion posters showed straw hats and airy off-the-shoulder dresses against seaside sunsets, I wore shabby old jackets I'd found in our basement before we moved. This was a mistake. Either you should be one of those who bothered about clothes and looked like everyone else, or one of those who never gave a thought to what you wore and put on any old trousers and jerseys. You shouldn't be like me. But anyway, my attitude worked in as far as it brought me some respect from other pupils. I became tough and inaccessible, someone whom not many dared approach. They stopped whispering about what I did or didn't do, or what I was like. They were impressed by my ability to stand outside everything and not do the usual teenage things in order to conform. Now I had acquired respect even from those who set the yardsticks for how you should be. I didn't realise they were slightly frightened of me, but just sensed I was being left alone in a way that was better for my self-esteem. I thought it was much better at school now than before, when I was being bullied. No one dared bully me any longer.

Of course, I was not politically minded, as I was never inclined towards groups in that way, and nor was I particularly familiar with world events. But intellectually it was quite clear to me which values I stood for, and if they had to be ascribed to some kind of ideology, they did not fall on the right. I thought other young people seemed very naive in the way they simply took over the values of their parents, with no understanding of the workings behind them. As I was not particularly close to my parents or to anyone else, my views had always been my own, not adjusted to what others thought. I couldn't imagine how it was that people seemed just to merge into others and other people's opinions, and formed their identities by thinking like other people. My sense of identity had always been clear, never connected with anyone else.

As I was now looking on the injustices of the world from various viewpoints, and analysing them in order to decide for myself which ethics and values I stood for, other people had little chance when I joined in on their discussions. I never initiated any, but if I got involved in a discussion I seldom regarded those with whom I was debating as worthy opponents. In discussion I never mixed things and people, which meant that those who did so appeared childish. I always said precisely what I thought. Usually, though, I let people go straight through me and ignored them.

Adults were sometimes easier to talk to, but there were not many of that kind in my life. Now and again someone like that would appear, but only unhappy, damaged people, adults telling me their sorrows, seeing something equal to them in my verbal maturity and my silent ability to listen. Perhaps I also became the recipient of confidences concerning the horrors in their lives; their emotional dust-bin, because they sensed that I never told anyone else what I had heard. I had no need to gossip, to tell people things. I had no competitive sense and no winning instinct, which made me reliable as a keeper of secrets. I didn't realise I was sometimes being used and exploited as a listener. I liked listening. It was easier than talking, and a good opportunity to try to learn something about people. Why did they do what they did? And what really was it that they were doing? I listened and pondered. I felt I could be of silent use to those I was listening to.

When it came to my mother, I didn't want to listen, but her words were always there whether I wanted to hear them or not: she was going to kill herself, and then we'd see all right that she didn't want to live any longer ... everyone was so horrible to her ... it was she who was taking the brunt of it all. When I got back from school, I sometimes stood at the front door and wondered whether today would be the day she had done it, whether she would be lying dead in there. I would think about it as I unlocked the door. I must be truly awful, I thought, not to be particularly miserable if she were dead. But a corpse would be beastly. She was spongy, puffy, swollen. Her corpse would be disgusting.

If she were dead, I thought, I wouldn't touch her. If her eyes were open, I wasn't going to close them. I had no intention of closing those eyes, as they did in films. And I hoped I would be alone with her then, when she was dead, so that no one saw me. So that no one saw that I was not unhappy. I would probably phone the police. I wouldn't need to phone for an ambulance because she would be stone-dead and I would know it. In that case my sister mustn't come home while I was waiting—if she did, she would be angry with me for not being miserable. Why didn't I care about my mother as Kerstin did? There *must* be something wrong with me.

I unlocked the door and thought—perhaps this is it. Perhaps she is dead. But she never was. She just became less and less a person. Sometimes there was a fire in the apartment when I got home, but never anything that I couldn't put out. Once she had put pizza cartons on the stove with all the hotplates switched on. I didn't know whether she had wanted to start a fire or whether she simply didn't know what she was doing. I threw a bucket of water on to the fire and tried to get rid of the smell of burnt cardboard that filled the whole apartment. I was tired and sad. I didn't want to go on. Death didn't frighten me, either my own or anyone else's. It felt as if I'd always had a bit of death inside me, as if knowing about being shut out and detached was to know something about death—having a preview of it.

My mother was living vomit creeping after me wherever I went, and I wanted to be free of her. I wanted to ease her off me. I wanted to be myself, in peace and alone. I was wretched because I couldn't understand this strange world, or what I should do in it. I occasionally turned over the idea of suicide, but that became intellectual, slightly detached thinking. I didn't want to live any longer, but I couldn't find any feeling relating to that thought. Where that, or the desire to live, should have been was nothing but a hole—a nothingness. The sense of wanting to die would have been necessary to drive me into any kind of action. That driving force didn't exist, though neither did the will to live. I was tired and empty.

My father had now disappeared completely. At first, after their divorce, he had come home a few times to fetch things. To come just to see Kerstin and me wouldn't have occurred to him. To him, people were always interchangeable, and he always exchanged them for people who provided him with the greatest profit at the time.

'You have children only until they're eighteen. I can't think about them now. I have to see to my own home,' he said to his new wife.

He had not even told her that he had any children at all, until just before they married. He had said he was getting a divorce, but as he had never mentioned any children she had taken it for granted there weren't any. I didn't find that out until he had separated from her as well. Then, a few years later, he exchanged even her—this time for a wife and children with even better odds. After a long period of what was as good as bigamy, after he had built a new life in another town, he came home one day and told his second wife he wanted to separate. 'I might just as well leave you before you leave me. I have to think about myself,' he had said.

She was shocked by his total coldness, and telephoned us. I was the one to answer the phone, and she poured it all out while I listened. I hardly had to say anything. I sounded like an adult when people talked to me, and I would sit wherever I was put, which made me a good recipient of other people's problems. I had any amount of patience, and never tired. My father's wife wanted me to go to her place, so I did. I felt useful—at least there was someone who had some use for me. She was one of those adults who allowed themselves to be deceived by my precociousness, and drew on my presence instead of seeking consolation from someone more of her own age. Later on, especially when they were slightly drunk, adults used to tell me about rapes, beatings, war experiences—things they said they had never told anyone else. I seemed to have some kind of calming effect on them, perhaps because I was never upset or surprised. By the time I was fifteen, I thought I'd heard and seen everything.

Thirteen

I needed some kind of fellowship, if for nothing else than to be on my own and to have somewhere to be. I didn't want to be at home, where my mother was in the process of regressing right back to the reptile era. I didn't want to see it.

I needed somewhere to go, and I gradually found the kind of companionship I was searching for among some people who smoked hash. As long as the joint or pipe was being handed round, I could be left to sit quietly and inside myself without anyone bothering me with more than a few passing comments.

'Cor, she's right stoned.'

'Christ, you're dead high, eh?'

Then I was left alone. I had no need to answer.

I was smoking hash and marijuana in order to acquire the right to be left on my own in the presence of other people. There was also another notion—a half-formed question. Had I too, the changeling, the ugly duckling, a place where I belonged? Was a pot-smoker what I was supposed to be? Were they my kind? It turned out they were not, but it was distinctly easier, with them, to pretend to be of the same kind.

I could also use hash as an excuse for some of my difficulties, although being high often emphasised my problems rather than easing them. Judging speeds and distances became even more difficult after I'd smoked hash, but if it took me a quarter of an hour longer to cross the street, I was able to tell myself that it was because I was so high. This made it easier, and I could suppress the fact that I found it difficult to cross the street even in ordinary circumstances. If there was any traffic at all, I had always taken great long detours to find crossings with traffic lights. I could never judge how fast the cars were going, or when I would be able to cross. Now I suppressed all that and instead became someone else, someone I understood, someone who was not inexplicable. I smoked this and became that—simple.

I also felt that if I behaved oddly in the eyes of other people, it was enough for me to be able to put the blame on the fact that I had been smoking hash. Just keeping that explanation to myself made it easier to bear. So in my loneliness I started smoking hash more and more frequently. I could sit with my pipe in a bush somewhere and then go around high all day, by myself.

Others enjoyed being high, but I never really understood the idea of it all. They sat together. They giggled. They listened to music and ate sweets. They made use of music to enjoy their euphoria. I just wanted to be left to my own devices, and although I went to the same parties and hung around with them by the underground station in the evenings, I never became one of them. They all had quite different histories, nothing like mine. They had fathers who had hanged themselves, brothers who had shot themselves, older sisters in Hinseberg women's prison. They had been abused, sent to reform schools, were on probation. They had mothers who were alcoholics, junkies, unemployed, prostitutes or on incapacity pensions. They had lived in foster homes from which they had run away. They were totally abandoned, or were being sought by both the police and the social services.

I found it liberating that no façades were scrubbed here, that people said things as they were, and I felt my mother's alcoholism somehow fitted in. But nonetheless I basically had a middle-class background, and that separated me from them. Although I learnt their language as easily as I took in foreign languages, I also had other languages, which they hadn't.

I found it difficult to mix and often just hung around with them, silently. Even here, my taciturnity combined with my deadly contemptuousness made an impression on other people. I was the one who seemed shy and stayed on the fringes of everything, I looked like a girl from a proper family. But at the same time I behaved in a contrary way. I saw no reason to take particular care of myself, and death did not frighten me. I stuffed myself with anything in the way of drugs, and I could drink just as much as the boys. The boys' way of mixing also seemed easier to adjust to. They didn't have that girlish, intrusive arm-in-arm manner that I didn't understand. But although they were mostly damaged and drug-fixated young people in this gang, they had closer relations with each other than I had with anyone. I felt I was always in some kind of state of emergency.

I had two desires in life—to understand myself and to be a real person. As the former seemed impossible, I tried the latter. A real person was normal, and this was what I was striving for. Normality included relationships, and I discovered that sex worked. I could have sex with anyone, for it required no special closeness. It became a way of having relations without having them, a way of making my life look more normal. If it was also destructive, this was the price I was prepared to pay in order to feel real. Using sex in this way was not difficult in a gang that consisted mostly of boys. Usually another girl and I were the only girls there. This other girl in the gang took the part of the one who held back. She was the pretty blonde whom everyone wanted but no one could have. She was the virgin, although she went to parties, drank and took as many drugs as anyone else. She was destructive, but elegant with it. So the promiscuous role was vacant, and it was I who was able to provide the *un*lovely destructiveness with a body. This meant acquiring an identity despite my silence.

When amphetamines—junk—came in as a new drug amongst the gang, there were many who backed out and thought beer and a joint were enough and you shouldn't go along with that kind of thing. But I tried it out immediately, without thinking twice. What would it matter a hundred years from now? I had nothing to lose.

The older boys sometimes warned me, saying I oughtn't to have anything to do with such things. The older ones showed consideration for the younger ones, rather than any real desire to tempt them into drugs. But their solicitousness passed me by. I took a whole lot of junk, sniffed it up my nose or drank it dissolved in water. I knew nothing about injecting it. But junk wasn't a drug that suited me. In contrast to other drugs, I had to take a lot of amphetamines to get high, and this also became very expensive. Furthermore, amphetamines were a social drug, a drug for mixing with people rather than for introversion, and they didn't suit me. I felt no special attraction to amphetamines and took them more and more rarely.

My maternal grandparents died, and one result was that my mother was left a large legacy, so now there was no financial obstacle to her need for pills and alcohol. To me, money was a very abstract and incomprehensible concept. I didn't realise that my mother was in fact quite rich, and the sum of money she had received was a very large one to devote to her addiction. Nor did I realise that, had she not inherited that money, the social services would have intervened in our life. My mother no longer worked, so there would have been no money for the rent. Dinners were no longer cooked at home. Each of us had to fend for food as best we could. I was fifteen and the hot-dog stall by the underground station was my dinner-table, the money filched from my mother's bag. Now there was no façade left for my sister to scrub. It had collapsed. Not even a semblance of home was left under the ruins.

Now and again my mother pulled herself together for a day and would be dressed when I arrived back from school. Having suddenly been out shopping and cooked a meal, she was now expecting me to eat it, pretending to ignore the vomiting, the spells of unconsciousness, of the last two weeks. Perhaps she was quite unaware of them. I thought her worse when she pretended to be a parent than when she was flat out in her room. And I simply couldn't eat what she had bought, she disgusted me so. She looked hurt when I refused to eat the food she had cooked. She looked as if she was thinking here she was, making an effort for an ungrateful brat. Her reaction was utterly absurd considering that she had probably not even been seen for a week, having been lying with her beer and vodka in her urine-smelling room behind the kitchen. But that didn't seem to worry her.

My mother's inheritance was not just money. My grandparents had possessed a whole lot of furniture and works of art. I was alone at home with my mother one day when the doorbell rang, and as she was drunk as usual and locked in her room, I opened the door. Outside were two men who said they had come from a removal firm. They brought in all the furniture from my grandparents' house. I hadn't even known they were coming.

They carried in all the cardboard boxes and objects and filled the whole apartment with all that furniture. They asked where they were to put everything, but I didn't know, so all they could do was to stack all the articles on top of each other. When they had finished, they wanted to be paid, but I had no money.

'I must wake my mother up,' I said, and went and thumped on her door.

'Go to hell!' she snapped from inside.

No other reaction. I tried again.

'Mother, wake up!'

'To hell with you,' she shouted.

I didn't know what to say to the removal men, who were standing in the next room, but they said they would go and get some lunch and come back in an hour for the money. An hour later, I had still not succeeded in getting my mother to give me any—I had no idea that I could have asked for a bill or something similar. When they came back, I made a last desperate attempt and banged on mother's door.

'You *must* give me some money.'

I could hear her moving in there this time.

'Christ Almighty, I suppose I'll have to come then, if they want their bloody money.'

I took a few steps towards the living-room where the men were waiting, and told them she was on her way. At that moment she came out of her room, stark-naked, stinking of stale booze and looking indescribably repugnant. She was holding a large bundle of unsorted banknotes in one hand, as if she had scooped them up from the floor.

'You want some money, do you? That's all you ever want, you fucking bloodsucker,' she said to me, slurring the words.

She took no notice whatsoever of the two strange men standing in the hall.

'Here you are, you bloody tart,' she shouted, flinging the bundle at me.

High-denomination banknotes rained down on me. This simply couldn't be true—this couldn't really be happening, could it? I couldn't take it in, it was so unreal, standing there with banknotes in my hair and two caught on the rough surface of my jersey. It was unreal, mother standing there naked and dirty, and the men looking away. I didn't know what to say or do—it was all so weird and nasty. I picked some notes up off the floor and gave them to the men, to make them go. I certainly didn't want any sickly pity from them. They had nothing to do with all this, or with me. They looked relieved to be able to get away.

I had no idea how profoundly contemptuous my mother's gesture had been. I had no sensors for the symbolic humiliation of throwing money at someone, or calling them a tart. This was the kind of thing my mother and father had done. It was painful and unpleasant to be exposed to it in the presence of those men, but though it distressed me I still didn't understand it. Perhaps, together with my innate ability to retreat into myself and stay there, it was this that contributed to my survival.

There were a lot of things I didn't know, simple everyday skills that I lacked. The older I grew, the more I learnt to zigzag in order to avoid them. This meant a great deal of energy went into thinking things out and always being one step ahead, trying to foresee the next thing so that I could swerve in time when approaching something unfamiliar. I didn't know why I was always so tired. I was trapped in a labyrinth in which one complicated path led into the next, and I never found any way out. I didn't see my difficulties because I was so busy trying to parry them. To strain to get an overall view, to understand what I didn't understand, would have required access to far more energy than I possessed. So I tried to get through the present as best I could.

I noticed that things often somehow got stuck when I talked to people, but I didn't know why. If someone asked me how I was, I replied without twigging that it was then my turn to ask. 'Fine.'

I didn't catch on that I was expected to say something other than just 'Fine'. I had no real sense for this kind of conversational exchange. I would have thought it simplest if at first *I* had said what I had to say, and then the other person had spoken. To keep hopping back and forth, trying to spot the right point to say something, was difficult and tiring. So I often seemed more nonchalant and uninterested than I really was. Or silence might fall if someone asked an indirect question.

'I'd like your phone number.'

'Oh yes,' I would reply at best to such a statement, if I said anything at all. It was just a statement, and I didn't realise it meant I should give the questioner my number.

'Can I have your telephone number?' he or she would perhaps say after a moment's silence.

'Yes,' I would reply again.

That was a wholly logical answer according to my way of seeing it—an answer to a question. But then there would be another silence. Not until someone asked the right question, the direct question, 'What's your telephone number?', did I reply with the number. I truly had not the slightest notion that people could mean anything but what they said; that 'I'd like your telephone number' really meant 'What is your telephone number?' But even if I didn't understand what was happening, I did feel the odd effects of it—that the conversation became somewhat halting, with a lot of peculiar silences.

I also found it difficult to fathom polite phrases, the kind you said just because you ought to, speech without content. And this contributed to the impression of bad manners others had of me. When I had learnt the phrase used to thank someone for food, and knew when I was expected to use it, I very rarely found the right moment. Sometimes I would say it while I was still eating, in order to have time to say it, and on other occasions I didn't say it at all because I couldn't quite remember when I should say it. For a long time, I also felt very uncertain about what was meant by food when you thanked someone for it. Was everything you ate food? Should you say the same when someone offered you an apple?

What was food?

There were things that certainly were food—sausages were food and meat was food. Was soup food? Soup was liquid. If soup was food, then perhaps tea also was food? Though there were solid bits in soup and there weren't any in tea. But what about porridge? How could you use that phrase when you weren't certain what food was?

Defining food was not my only problem at mealtimes. My table manners were not that good, and I couldn't take the skin off boiled potatoes. As I didn't know how to do it, at school I ate the potatoes with the skin on. There was always a very unappetising rough spotted skin on school potatoes, and no one else ate it. But if anyone commented on the fact that I ate potato skin, which they did occasionally, I just said the skin was good for you.

I usually ate alone, as I didn't have any friends at school. One day, just when I had sat down in the school dining-room, a girl in my class came and sat at my table. We were eating late that day and there was hardly anyone left in the dining-room. I didn't know her and had hardly ever spoken to her, although she was in my class.

'You can't skin potatoes, can you?' she said.

She was just stating quite matter-of-factly that I couldn't, without implying anything else. I didn't have to answer. It didn't matter that she had said that. I didn't feel hurt.

'I'll show you how,' she said, and she took my hands and showed me step by step what to do.

It was an important moment for me—although she almost certainly forgot it soon afterwards—because it was the first time anyone had understood intuitively what it was I couldn't do and how I needed to be instructed in order to learn how. I didn't really find it difficult to learn, but the reason why I hadn't been able to skin potatoes before was that just explaining in words was not enough for me. Nor was it enough just to look on. I had to learn with my own hands, one step at a time. Of course, I had a great many other problems, and being unable to master the art of skinning potatoes was perhaps not one of the greatest. Anyway, now I didn't have to eat those unappetising potato skins. My classmate's friendly and instructive interest surprised me, but also warmed me.

I still found it difficult to tolerate changes and surprises, but my ritualistic behaviour was now a thing of the past, and I no longer needed to take certain routes and touch certain things. The only vestige of this kind was a sort of compulsive clearing of my throat, a sound half-way between clearing my throat and swallowing. I was aware of these sounds—in contrast to the more unconscious sounds I had made when I was small—and I suffered from not being able to stop them. But I did in fact have a reason for them. As I sometimes couldn't speak, and couldn't get a word out, even when inside me I was trying to, by making these little sounds I was able to check that I did in fact still have a voice.

I didn't know why I was sometimes shut off or why I didn't always answer when spoken to—I just noticed that it was so. When I didn't succeed in connecting with my nervous system so as to make my voice carry out the order to speak that I had given it, it felt as if my voice had disappeared. I was worried that one day I wouldn't have any voice at all, that I wouldn't be able to speak to anyone ever again, so I made that little sound all the time. I did it to reassure myself that my voice was still there. Perhaps the sound also helped to keep my nervous system active, so that I didn't slide back into myself.

At school I represented myself at parents' meetings and such like. I thought that logical and perfectly all right. My parents had nothing to do with me and I didn't miss them there. But it did sometimes feel rather odd sitting among other people's parents, waiting for my turn to speak to whichever teacher it happened to be. If anyone made any comment, I ignored it. I didn't have to lie about why my parents weren't there. People liked putting the words into my mouth. They asked questions, then answered themselves with acceptable explanations.

I was able to let people and their comments blow right through me like a wind without even a breeze disturbing a hair, or else wash through me like a wave without a drop of water touching me. As if at the very moment their words might make contact with me, I simply changed density for a moment. But I couldn't always choose when that would happen, so it was not a technique that could protect me from having painful feelings. It was a way of protecting my sensitive system from being overloaded with incomprehensibles rather than from the actual feelings, either mine or those of others.

Gym, always really difficult, now became even more humiliating because of the teacher's well-meaning methods. Basically, I could do none of the things expected of me, and I didn't dare do much anyway because I sensed I might harm myself if I knew neither how my body was put together nor how it related to the gym itself. But our teacher was young and she thought she had a good method for poor pupils. Every lesson, she appointed two pupils to help anyone who found it difficult, and if there was anything they simply couldn't manage, the two had to work with that pupil. The 'anyone' was always me, and the exercise would consist of rolling a large ball between us in a corner of the gym. So I almost always found myself in that corner, with the ball. Alternatively, they would lower or change all the apparatus, and hold on to me when it was my turn. There were others in the class who sometimes couldn't manage something, but I was the only one who never managed anything to the same standard as the others.

I felt a total failure, as if I was physically handicapped but everyone was pretending I wasn't. The very fact that other pupils had to help me I found mortifying. Gym had always been a torment. I'd got used to this, but that others now had to help me I found extremely degrading. Other people's good intentions were always harder for me to deal with emotionally than their dislike or anger. Well-meaning actions were painful, because they were always wrong in some way; no one ever saw my real problems.

After I'd tried everything I could think of, my last resort was to refuse. I stopped joining in, but I didn't stop going to the lessons. Without changing, I would go and sit on a bench and watch. The teacher was very cross with me. She considered she had really done a great deal for me, and she also thought she was a good gym teacher, not one of the tough old school. She thought she created an atmosphere of equality in the gym, an atmosphere in which it was not *being* the best, but just joining in and all of us *doing* our best, that was most important. But I had no explanation for my clumsiness. I had no why to offer. Although I ought not to be, I was just clumsy and uncertain, and the gym teacher's methodology was no help to me.

To her, I became a personal defeat—if it wasn't always my own fault that I needed help, then it was certainly my own fault that I was not helped by the help offered to me. It had to be that. Now she *had* to get me to join in, not for my sake any longer, but for the sake of her own reputation as a teacher. But this had no effect. If I refused, I flatly refused. I tried to evade all conversations, all the 'Now you really must . . .' gambits, and all her threats of zero marks. I made myself slippery in order to slide past, and I developed this slipping away into a fine art. I often succeeded in being a step ahead of the adults, so that just as they were drawing breath to tell me to stay, or that they wanted to speak to me, I got a whiff of something in the air and slid past the second before they had time to say it. Although in other areas I had a fairly poor sense of timing, I acquired one here. I rapidly learnt to interpret

a sigh, an intake of breath, or a step in my direction—
they were the adults' way of collecting themselves, perhaps
smoothing their hair, frowning slightly or clearing their
throats just before they had to deal with something
troublesome—with me. As if reading their thoughts, I
would dematerialise myself just as they were about to put
a hand on my shoulder.

In middle school, needlework had been a quiet refuge.
In senior school, it was much more problematical. Now
we were to make clothes, using sewing-machines. I could
no longer sit in a corner fiddling with something small.
Again, it was difficult for me to take in all the instructions
and to remember them.

Copy the pattern, trace it, draw it out . . . a seam allow-
ance, a tuck here and a tuck there. Cutting the material,
sewing it. Pressing both sides, hemming, interfacing with
vilene. Vilene . . . that was an interesting word, a lovely
word. Cutting, pressing, making a tuck.

I couldn't keep all these bits in my head, and if I asked,
the teacher said I hadn't been listening properly. She had
no doubt of it. At first I often came to a halt in the middle
of something and didn't know what I was doing. The noise
of the sewing-machines went right into me, too, vrrr, vrrr,
clackety-clackety-clack, vrrr, vrrr. The sound didn't make
me lose my foothold as other sounds did, but I simply
couldn't shut it out. It was louder than I could have imagined and it exhausted me, as if it were a battle between
me and the noise, in which I tried to hold out my arms
and push it away from me with the palms of my hands. It
pressed in on me all the time—vrrr, clackety-clack—
vibrating and pushing against my outstretched hands. As
soon as my arms tired and sagged a bit, the sound took
over the whole of me.

All the time, I had actively to keep it away from me, at
the same time setting up a boundary, a kind of inner

barrier, between the part of my mind devoting itself to shutting out the noise and the part that had to concentrate on cutting the piece of cloth I was holding. And I had to keep guard on the boundary there. If one side leaked over into the other, I was utterly lost.

So what with these four simultaneous tasks, I hadn't all that much energy left. If another sewing-machine then started up—another sound to fend off—keeping that sound out was another separate activity, until I had added it to the sound of the first sewing-machine and made it into a single one. Not until then could I use one and the same force to keep both sounds out. But my energy ran out, and I couldn't do it. I hadn't enough 'inner hands' to resist it all. My inner fuse-box was overloaded and the mains switch was now off. My senses did indeed remain in operation—I saw, I heard and I felt, but I no longer took anything in. My hearing was still there rattling away in my ear, but it didn't get through to me, nor could I fetch it. My sight sat on my retina as clearly as anything. As this was my sharpest, most reliable and most easily manipulated sense, I could actually choose to take in a little bit of it, but the rest I left there behind my eye. What I could see always penetrated most easily, even when the plug had been pulled on the system. What I felt, on the other hand, was simply outside my body, and if I had itched somewhere, in a way I would have known, but I would have had no reason to go there and fetch the itch so it didn't affect me.

Needlework lessons became something to be suffered, although actually I rather liked sewing. I just sat there, screened off from myself, with something I ought to do in front of me. Or else I would wander aimlessly around, trying to keep myself going and looking at what the others were doing.

Fourteen

I was relieved when my middle school days were over. I didn't know what lay ahead of me, nor was I all that interested. Although it felt good to be leaving middle school, I had nevertheless applied to go on to the senior part. I really did want to study, and amazingly enough I still had some desire to learn left, though how I would manage three more years at school I simply couldn't imagine. But whatever it was going to be like, could it possibly be worse than the nine years of anguish I had just gone through?

At the end of term, lots of parents came to the ceremonies, and in the senior school next door Kerstin had just taken her final exams. My father and the aunts were there with presents for her. Kerstin was clever and had worked hard at school. Neither my father nor the aunts could be bothered to walk the two hundred metres to see me at my end-of-term ceremonies. I had done nothing praiseworthy, or even interesting. I wasn't musical, I hadn't been confirmed, I wouldn't be taking finals and I wasn't polite, caring or well mannered. I was not a real person.

I was given my report and stuffed it into my pocket. When I got out on to the school yard, groups of pupils and parents were standing around everywhere. I walked past them and across to the park, where the class was to assemble afterwards. I was the first there, so I went behind some bushes and smoked a joint. When the others in the class arrived, I sat with them. I had with me some vodka from the inexhaustible supply in my mother's wardrobe.

Some of the others were drinking beer, and all of them were opening their reports to see their marks. I didn't really like being drunk, but it was a way of being there while not being inexplicably different or odd. It was also a way of being self-electedly different, because I was the one who had the strongest drink and who would drink the most.

I didn't open the envelope with my marks in it until long afterwards, as I was not particularly curious about what they were. It turned out to be a fairly unusual leaving report—I had three top marks, one just below, and the rest near the bottom, then a line which meant no marks at all for gym.

Now that Kerstin had taken her final exams, she was quick to leave home, as far away from home as she could possibly get. She went to Italy. So I was now living alone with my mother, and things became more and more difficult. When my sister had been there, my mother had at least had some inhibitions left, but now she let them all go. She was frightened of me.

Deep down, somewhere beyond her drinking and her pills, she was afraid of me, and what frightened her was that the only really strong feeling she had managed to instil in me was a colossal indifference. I didn't realise that was so. I was alone and stripped bare, while she drenched me with her contempt. I knew nothing of the mechanisms of hatred and contempt, and thought that if you didn't like someone, you just didn't bother about them. But my mother spewed malice all over me.

'You're ugly and disgusting,' she would say to me. 'No man will ever want you.'

She pushed me around and slapped me with her sticky hands. I tried to keep her out of my room, to be left alone. It was as if I had, in our own apartment, a large distasteful animal I was trying all the time to shove out of my way.

'You're so ugly you'll never get a man. You cheap fat slut! Think yourself clever, do you? You're nothing but a disgusting brat. You can go to hell. No one will ever want you,' she screamed.

I tried to ignore her, but when I didn't answer, she would just go on. 'You're a total failure. You're fat and ugly and a failure.'

Whenever I didn't know what to do, I put on my out-door clothes and went out. I just wanted to get away. But she would go on shouting while I was getting dressed.

'Go on, just go, go out and see if there's anyone who wants you, if there's anyone who wants a pathetic fat six-teen-year-old! Do that, go on! To hell with you. Don't think I'll help you with anything. Go to hell, you damned brat! Go and sleep on the streets.'

When I closed the door, she would shout through it. 'D'you think you'll ever get a man the way you look! Fat and freckled and revolting!'

She kept on like that. It never stopped. I heard it day after day—how awful and repulsive I was—but I did not grasp the depths of contempt my mother held me in. I didn't understand the emotion she framed her words in, but the concrete message was sufficiently clear. And as it was when she was conscious that she poured it all out over me, I preferred her when she was flaked out.

I just wanted to leave home and be left to myself. To be grown up, to move out and be left to my own devices. I had only the vaguest idea that other sixteen-year-olds had other lives and other dreams. I wanted to be left on my own and be a real person. I often showed my mother how indifferent I was. I would shrug and walk away. But sometimes, according to my logic, I confronted her quite straightforwardly. When she talked about not wanting to live any longer, when she said she wanted to take her own life, I opened the balcony door for her.

'Go on them, jump,' I would say calmly.

If she had jumped, it would have been a relief—some disgust and unpleasantness with all the blood, but mostly relief. I didn't hate her. She simply didn't arouse sufficient emotion in me for that. I just thought it would be simplest if she died. She wanted to die. She said she did. And I wanted to be left in peace, to escape her, to be alone. The useless, distasteful life she lived couldn't be worth having. So it would be better if she actually died, if she took her own life as she kept saying she would do—then things would be calmer. But she didn't. She never jumped off the balcony, she never took all her pills, she never threw herself under an underground train. She just said she would. Why didn't she mean what she said? I never understood.

My need to get away from home grew even greater. When the time came to go to senior school, starting there was already inconceivable. If I was to move away from home I would have to get a job. But I didn't know what working meant, or how to set about getting a job. I was unemployed, and life became even emptier. No one cared whether I existed, or what I did. I wasn't needed for anything. Everything seemed meaningless and I cared neither about myself nor about the world. I grew my own marijuana, smoked it and slept.

Now that I no longer automatically received food at school, I started eating irregularly. I didn't know how often one ought to eat—no cooked meals had been seen at home for years. I would jiggle open the lock of my mother's door when she was out for the count, in order to steal money from her handbag to be able to buy something to eat. She would be lying there on her bed, looking brain-dead, corpse-white, bruises all over her legs and arms—dead, though alive. Her hair would be one great untidy mess on the top of her head and her room smelt decayed and acrid, a soft rotten smell mixed with the acid smell of the alcohol. Newspapers and beer cans lay all over the floor. Unwashed mugs and spewed-on towels. A bucket she had peed in. Empty bottles—Explorer Vodka and Silver Rum. In the open wardrobe was a store of unopened bottles of spirits, perhaps twenty of them. She kept her handbag in bed with her, and held on to it. When I needed money I would pull it slowly out of her grasp and open it. In it were high-denomination bank-notes. I would take one big one as there were still a lot left, and put the bag back beside her. On my way out, I might pick up a bottle of Silver Rum from her wardrobe. She might notice, but then again she might not. Anyhow, there was nothing she could do about it. I was quicker, soberer and stronger than she was.

I had no discernible feeling of being hungry, or not. I didn't know what I ought to eat. I didn't know how to cook anything, and sometimes I ate nothing at all. A pan-cake-type roll of soft thin bread or a pizza was the only cooked food I ate. Otherwise, crisps and Coca Cola were what I might have for breakfast, lunch or dinner. When-ever I forgot to eat, I would live on coffee and cigarettes for several days.

My mother was often paranoid and thought I was out to get her. Sometimes she would collect up all the tele-phones and lock them into her room because she thought I was phoning people in order to talk about her. I just did what seemed appropriate, and worked out a way of getting into her room to fetch a telephone if I needed one. Or I would hide the telephones before she took them. I didn't ponder on what was mentally sick and what was normal, I just adapted to the prevailing circumstances.

I very seldom had temper tantrums now. They had become more frequent when I was twelve or thirteen— then I had screamed, bitten and thrown things about if anyone tried pushing me into a situation I couldn't cope with. After that they had gradually disappeared, as I became more and more exhausted and detached from everything. But now something happened that completely convinced me that I must leave home at once—I physically abused my mother.

One evening I was talking on the phone to someone, perhaps one of the few occasions when my father rang. Suddenly, she came out of her room and over to me. Her eyes had that paranoid look, and her movements were jerky and rigid. Staring at me, and without saying anything, she pulled the telephone plug out of the socket so that our conversation was broken off, then snatched at the phone. She was to have the telephones, all of them, and immediately. But I wrenched the phone out of her hands and threw it back at her, hitting her on the head. I hadn't thought, it just happened. As the phone hit her, she fell to the floor like a log, and stayed there. When I bent over her to see if she was alive, she clawed at my face. Something inside me happened then. I didn't know what I was doing, but I grabbed her by the hair and banged her head on the floor. It was easy, as if her head was loose on her neck. I went on banging until a pool of blood appeared on the parquet floor under her head. My hand seemed to do it automatically. I wasn't thinking or feeling anything, just reacting.

Afterwards, I was frightened. I had practically never hurt anyone before, and I didn't want to be a person who hurt people. I was frightened for myself, and more disgusted at having held her dirty, greasy hair and having her blood on me than I was worried about whether she was alive. I realised I had to move out.

That autumn I met Jon. He had an apartment, and I needed somewhere to live. I supplied him with my home-grown grass and we soon became a couple. I moved into

184

his little flat. I was sixteen, he seventeen. I had no idea about work, finances, no concept of bills or rents. I hadn't a clue about how all that worked. Jon was not excessively pleased about me moving in with him, but I was prepared to adapt to anything to escape having to go back home. I could be anyone—someone else or no one at all—as long as I didn't have to live at home. Jon pointed that out to me. He said I was only living with him to escape having to live at home, but I strenuously denied it. He was right, but I didn't know it—I was simply trying to survive.

By living with someone I was trying to be a real person, but I didn't know how to have a relationship. I didn't know what the point was or what it was you were supposed to do with the man you were together with. I grew more and more silent, more and more detached. I didn't grasp at all what it meant just to be with each other, what other couples seemed to do. The ability to manage this kind of arrangement didn't seem to exist in me. My system just had 'on' and 'off', no intermediate setting. Sometimes I turned quite mute and couldn't speak. Maybe I was silent no more often than I'd been before, but it became so much more obvious now that I was sharing my life with another person. My failings showed up in sharp relief against the backdrop of Jon's abilities. And my weaknesses also aroused his sadistic tendencies. He would be annoyed by everything I did, and vent his irritation on me. I just accepted everything; and, in particular—the fact that I didn't even appear to register his nastinesses—seemed to make the sadist in him emerge more and more often. But I got used to it, and on the whole life was fairly tranquil and good, as I saw it. I didn't know much about what a good life could be. Everything that wasn't like being at home with my mother was good.

Jon and I had a kind of comradeship, but there was no real warmth or closeness. Again, I didn't miss that part of our relationship, because I didn't know what it was. I just had a diffuse sense of emptiness.

'You're like a piece of furniture,' Jon said. 'You do nothing on your own initiative. You can be shoved around anywhere . . . You're not like a human being. You're like an object.'

He was perhaps right about that. But all the same, from our relationship I learnt some new things about the world. I learnt how to be grown up. I learnt about bills and rents. And above all, I entered a new world of books. I had always read a lot, but on Jon's bookshelves were books I'd never seen before. Books that had inside them things I had no idea about. I read everything he had—Sartre, Dostoevsky, Kafka and Camus—and I saw myself in them. In them were outsiderness, anguish, loneliness and aeons of emptiness. Not quite my kind of emptiness, but none-theless these were other worlds that seemed to be like mine. I read Charles Bukowski, William Burroughs and Jack Kerouac; they didn't exactly describe my reality, but they were concrete and straightforward, not avoiding what was ugly. I liked the fact that they wrote about things as they were.

Jon smoked quite a lot of hash, but it began to make me feel ill, so I stopped. He didn't like that, because in his eyes I had been the fixer. I had been the one who could get hash or grass whenever we needed it; that was the role I had had when I entered Jon's world. But now I had no more contacts. I'd slipped out of the gang as unnoticed as when I had joined it. I presumed that no one had noticed that I'd gone. I had no telephone number to get a fix, as I hadn't known any of them that well. I'd been able to buy stuff before only because I'd hung around and met the right people. I lived in town now, and hadn't been out to that suburb since moving here. The sales pitches out there varied, and I no longer had any idea where to go to get hash. I realised Jon would have liked me to be different, that he had thought I was someone else. He occasionally told me what I should be like, but I didn't know what to do to be like that.

He put an end to our affair several times, but I clung on. I had nothing else in the world, no family, nowhere to go. I tried obliterating myself so that he would put up with having me there. I needed him for practical reasons. I needed him for a roof over my head and in order to be a real person. When we were living together, I could work out how much and how often one should eat. I simply ate what he ate and thought it great to know how much was enough. Jon became a yardstick against whom I could measure myself. But he didn't want to be a yardstick—he thought I was empty, dull and lacking in will. He teased me for being afraid of things, for being clumsy and for never daring to try anything new. I worked hard at hiding my difficulties. I wanted to be a real person in his and in my own eyes—someone who wasn't peculiar, someone who was capable and bold. And I tried imitating others in order to be someone else—someone better.

We were terribly young, but I felt old and tired. We were both pretending to be adults. As Jon had lived in an apartment of his own for a while, he could teach me everything about how to manage on your own. We read his chosen books out loud and cooked vegetarian food. He had said that not a single piece of meat was to cross his threshold, so I adapted and became a vegetarian. There were also similarities between us that brought us closer together. Jon's father, like my mother, was an alcoholic. Sometimes we were woken at night by his father or my mother ringing up and yelling slurred words at us. Jon didn't want to pull the plug. I didn't understand why, but he liked his father in a way I had never liked my mother.

I met Jon's mother a few times. After we had been to see her the first time, Jon told me that she didn't like me. This didn't worry me particularly. I didn't need everyone to like me. Next time we went there for dinner, I told her I had heard she didn't like me and that she shouldn't worry, as I probably wouldn't be living with her son for ever. I didn't know that one shouldn't say such things. She looked strange and fell silent, but I had intended nothing more than what I had said—that she shouldn't worry about her son choosing someone she didn't approve of. I didn't think I'd be with Jon for ever. I noticed I'd said something stupid, but didn't know why it was stupid.

I had got a job in a grocery store, but I didn't like it much. Heavy milk and soft-drink crates had to be carried, goods had to be unpacked, and the cardboard boxes they were in had to be opened with a knife. I was no good with knives and kept cutting myself. The only thing I liked doing in the shop was sorting things and putting them in neat rows on the shelves.

Jon had a cleaning job, and as the apartment we lived in was small and cheap we had plenty of money, at least by my standards. We would often go out to the pub and drink wine, and I found it easier to pretend to be normal when I was slightly tipsy. Although we weren't really even old enough to be served alcohol, we tried to be an adult couple.

In the end, nothing helped. I could no longer make the effort. Jon was tired of me and I would have to move out. I was wretched and didn't know where to go. I had just got a day nursery supply job, which meant that I would be rung up in the morning and told which nursery I'd be working at. I didn't know how things would go with the job if I had nowhere to live and no telephone. So I went off desperately in search of somewhere to live. To move back home to my mother was unthinkable.

With some help from my father, I eventually got hold of a sublet apartment. I hadn't had any contact with him for a long time except for a regular maintenance cheque of 736 kronor a quarter. I phoned him at work and told him I had nowhere to live, and he suddenly rose to the occasion and procured an apartment owned by some acquaintance of his. So I now had a flat in Upplandsgatan, but no furniture, no crockery, nothing. A kind of home, but with nothing in it. My father gave me a box of dirty old aluminium saucepans he'd bid for at an auction. He was proud of getting them so cheaply and said I should get some steel wool to clean them. He had just bought triple glazing for his own home, Chinese matting and a new freezer, but I didn't give his meanness a second thought. I bought the steel wool, cleaned the pans and tried to manage on my own. Anyway, I did have a telephone and could be phoned.

I hadn't chosen the job for any special reason. Anyone could get work in day nurseries. But I found out that I worked very well with children and that I had an innate talent with them. I was concrete, clear and calm. I had endless patience. I never felt personally attacked by any child and I never got cross. I found it easy to set clear limits and be the same person without changing from one day to the next. I had no shifts of mood or days when I was easily irritated. On the whole, I was evenly the same. I was as if made for insecure children, so it turned out that I mostly worked with them. They headed for me, and although I was immature on many levels, I was adult in relation to children.

After a spell of being on supply in various places, I stayed on at one day nursery that needed staff. But although it was easier to be in the same place, the environment was terribly demanding. I had no good explanation to offer for why it exhausted me so, but there was always noise and movement, a mass of people, and I found it muddling and tiring. Being there sucked all the strength out of me, although I liked being with the children so much. A lot of minor things turned into burdens. When morning assemblies included the ring-game 'This ring is to wander', I would go to the cloakroom to escape joining in. I couldn't explain to anyone that I couldn't touch jewellery, and was almost unaware of it myself. I just tried to arrange life in such a way that I wouldn't have to face things I couldn't bear. I felt peculiar in an obscure way—all my evasions took up so much of my energy. Why couldn't I be a real person? Why couldn't I have an ordinary job, an ordinary apartment, an ordinary life?

One autumn morning, I was to open up the nursery, which meant I had to be there at half past six to let the first children in. I left home at about six and walked down the hill towards the bus stop at Odenplan. In the distance I could see a small crowd gathered round the hot-dog kiosk. By then it was ten past six and the air was clear but cold. I could see someone doing something by the kiosk, and everyone was staring. At the bus stop, the bus queue had turned into a semi-circle of spectators. I came a little nearer.

There was a woman by the kiosk. I could see her better now. She was wearing a blue dress, and my first thought was that I had had a dress exactly like that. The woman was screaming and yelling, but I still couldn't hear what. She was going round banging and crashing on the closed kiosk. As I got nearer and nearer, I thought: that woman looks like my mother. I took another step—it *was* my mother. There was my mother banging on the kiosk, in my old sleeveless dress, barefoot and with no outdoor clothes on. Then I heard what she was yelling. 'Come on out of there you bastards! I can hear you fucking in there.'

She was throwing stones at the kiosk, cursing and swearing. It was all very unreal. I walked past the passive onlookers and went over to her.

'Oh, hello, just as well you came,' she said, apparently not in the slightest bit surprised at my sudden appearance. 'Your father's in there, you see,' she said, pointing at the kiosk. 'He's taken all my things. They're in there, they've

190

cheated me!' She thumped the kiosk again with her clenched fists.

'Where have you been?' I asked her. The spectators were very close to us, looking as if they didn't want to miss a thing.

'Oh,' she said in a loud voice, 'I was in some pub somewhere, but I masturbated on a table and they threw me out.'

I was nineteen, and I didn't know why I didn't die on the spot. I pushed her down on to a bench and told her to stay there. Her eyes looked strangely childish and gleaming.

'I promise I won't move an inch,' she said, smiling and nodding like an obedient child.

I went back to my apartment, fetched some shoes and a coat, then went to the cash dispenser, took out some money and hurried back. I had to get to work on time, I kept thinking. I was always punctual. If I started work at half past six, I had to be there at half past six. I always did what I was told. I didn't think there were occasions when one didn't have to obey the rules.

My mother had her apartment keys in the dress pocket, so after I had got her into the coat and the too-large shoes, I put her in a taxi and told the driver where to take her. Then I went to work. But she couldn't be allowed to be like this—I had to do something, I thought. I also had a vague feeling that I was the one who had driven her to this madness. Perhaps I had made her like this. After work, I went to see her. I didn't really know why. I just felt I ought to.

There I was, in her apartment, now full of rubbish and newspapers. I sat there as she talked incessantly about sex, and I found it coarse and vulgar and revolting just listening to her. She heard voices and sounds everywhere. She said there were children crying under the floor of the lavatory and the neighbours were fucking in all the apartments round about. She was paranoid and didn't want to let me go. She locked the door and took the key so that I couldn't leave. I had never seen her like this before and I didn't know where to turn.

I phoned Kerstin and asked her what I ought to do with my mother. Kerstin had come back to Sweden, but didn't want to have anything to do with the family. I hadn't seen her for several years.

'Take her to the psych clinic,' she said, and put down the receiver.

I located a nearby psychiatric out-patient clinic in the telephone directory, and phoned them. They said my mother could go there. But they said nothing about what I had to do in order to get her there, nothing that would help me. They just said that I should make sure she ate something. After a great deal of persuasion, using food as a pretext, I managed to get her to open the front door and come out with me. I sat with her in a suburban pizzeria while she carried on ceaselessly about what she'd been hearing and seeing. She spoke in a loud voice about how they were having sex in the apartment above the pizzeria; she was pleased people could hear what she had to say. I felt as if I were taking part in an absurd film.

I walked with her to the clinic, as taking a bus or going by underground didn't seem very tempting; the pizzeria had been public enough.

'It's only delirium,' they said cheerfully at the out-patients. 'We'll put her down for aversion therapy. We'll give her an appointment for a few weeks' time.'

Thank you. Goodbye.

My mother was on a chair, hallucinating, and no one helped me phone for a taxi, no one gave me any advice on what I should do, no one asked whether I was all right. No one asked me if I had any money or whether I could manage to get her home. Our appointment was over and we no longer existed.

Before this incident, I had had no contact with my mother for a long time. But now she started telephoning me saying she was going to kill herself, or she would pour out a whole stream of invective about how awful I was. Those phone calls took up all my remaining energies. I listened to how foul I was, how disgustingly fat and awful, and I gave up any idea of a life. Life was not for me. I had no strength left, not for anything.

I could hardly cope with work any longer—I hadn't the energy to sort out my sensory impressions in those surroundings. It became too much for me to attempt to keep all those people apart and concentrate on whatever I was doing in a room full of children running about, jumping and yelling. Every day when I'd finished work, I went home, closed the door behind me, and slept. I was totally finished. I did the best I could at work, then there was nothing left.

I was often ill and had minor accidents. I cut myself. I twisted my ankles and cracked a bone in one of them. My body kept saying it couldn't cope, but I didn't understand why it couldn't. I was young. I ought to be able to work, like anyone else. It had to be because I was lazy, just as everyone had always said. It had to be my own fault that I failed at everything, that I had no life. The will to live had withered in me. I hadn't the strength to wish for anything any longer, except possibly to be away from everything. I had wanted to be left in peace, but I hadn't wanted that no one should care about me. I hadn't wanted to be alone and with no family. My life was so empty, it echoed as I moved around in it.

Fifteen

At some time or other over recent years I had tried most things in the drug line, but had not been all that addicted to anything. I mostly thought it didn't much matter but I might as well try stuff out—which had meant I'd taken anything that had come my way. It seemed easier to meet people doing this kind of thing than meeting people in other contexts. But now I was tired and miserable; I felt that I could manage no more and that I had failed at everything I'd undertaken. I was peculiar, and there was no prospect of things getting better. No one cared about what happened to me, so why should I bother about them?

I met Annie. She lived a life of devastation, and I went with her into a world that was new to me. This was no suburban misery. Her world was one of illegal clubs, of slipping past queues and doing drug deals in pub toilets. I tagged along. It was easy to be quiet and observant in these surroundings. All you had to do was to hang around at bar counters and disappear into the crowd. Annie was also an odd person. She had hardly any friends but masses of acquaintances. She had a reputation for being provocative, half-crazed and aggressive, and a lot of people who didn't know her knew who she was. She always found people to support her, in various ways, people who paid her drink bills and bought her things for a while and then were gone.

I could see that Annie was terribly frayed inside, and I seemed to provide some kind of stability in her life. I would stay wherever anyone put me. I wasn't like other girls. I didn't compete, had no competitive instinct. I had no need for attention. Perhaps Annie was better able to bask in her exhibitionist tendencies when she had me as a background. To me she was someone who offered a way of life at that particular time. I just let what happened happen. I needed a life, any old life.

Annie hit on the idea that we should go abroad, so we went to Spain. I had nothing to lose, nothing to care about—I just upped and went. I who found new surroundings so difficult wasn't even bothered about that now. I just wanted to get away. We ended up in a suburb of Barcelona, where Annie, as usual, quickly got to know people. She found it easy to make new acquaintances and to talk to people. Her new friends had plenty of drugs, of course, and they cost practically nothing. I was just there, in the middle of it all.

I still wanted to be a real person and I still thought that if only I could be one of a couple, it would make me seem more normal. With whom didn't really matter. I didn't know how to choose, so I chose Miguel, the dirtiest and most down-at-heel man I had ever seen. He was another oddball; the people in the neighbourhood treated him like a stray dog. They said he was dangerous, that I should watch out. I thought he might suit me.

I then lost contact with Annie and slipped into Miguel's world, the world of heroin. He was self-destruction personified, and notorious even among the heroin addicts—there were no limits to how low he would sink for a fix. Miguel once spent hours begging someone to give him a little heroin on credit. He would sell it, he said, then pay for it in arrears. When he finally managed to persuade the person to hand it over, and had been given some small white envelopes containing heroin, he went home and took them all. Then he had to face the consequences, so he took out a knife and slashed himself in the thigh. He went back to the person he'd had the heroin from with blood pouring down his leg and said he had been robbed. He reeled off the whole story, long and detailed, about how the robbers had stabbed him in the leg, the blood pouring out meanwhile. Not until then did he tie a rag round his leg and get a lift to hospital to have fifteen stitches put in it. For a free beer, Miguel was capable of sinking to the depths of degradation, without it bothering him. People just seemed to leave him cold. We had something in common—that lack of concern.

But Miguel also had something in common with both my mother and my father: he had my mother's propensity for degradation and my father's violence. Sometimes I was beaten up, and I was surprised by the force there could be behind a punch. I had thought it was for effect that people flew through the air in fights in films. Now I realised that it wasn't a trick. It also surprised me that you actually did see stars like in the comics, or at least dancing lights, after a few swift punches to the head. Pain still didn't bother me, though.

I didn't understand the driving force that heroin appeared to be. I lacked all driving force, the kind other people seemed to have. I wanted to understand it and I wanted to have it. I wanted an engine, something to work me up, which would drive me towards a goal, any goal. I wanted to learn to be a real person. I recognised that the only way to investigate that driving force was to throw myself into dependency.

The first couple of times I injected heroin I just felt sick, and nothing of the actual ecstasy tempting me to go on. My stomach turned inside out and I vomited into every bush I passed. But I was determined to understand this. In some vague way, I knew that it was actually my own development I was working on, if only in an inverted and harmful way. The third time, I experienced the kick. I felt the heroin rising like a rocket, striking the top of my skull with a dull clang, then spreading like a fan and trickling down into my body. Now I had some idea of what drove people into doing almost anything for this drug. But only an inkling. I was not yet addicted.

As addicts go, I was not a good subject. Other addicts seemed to have iron physiques, and I hadn't. I was sensitive to poisons. I had a weak body and could hardly find a vein to inject into. I still had my baby fat, more or less, and my circulation had always been poor. I usually had to dip my hands into hot water and then inject into the veins on the backs of them. I stuck a great many holes in myself before hitting the right place, but I knew I had to get into addiction in order to understand it. It took a while before I could inject enough into me, and often enough, for my body to start shrieking for heroin, but it did in the end. Even then I stood with one foot outside, analysing the situation. I kept seeing what abstinence was like, and how you could let it steer your behaviour. I could see what it could be like to possess a will somewhere in your intellect. I had never experienced that before, and I needed to take strong stuff like this to feel it. I acquired knowledge on what a driving force is. I felt a longing to repeat that kick just once more, together with an indescribable physical feeling that only a fix could make my body function. I wondered what this new dependency would drive me to do? Prostitute myself? I gave it a thought, but no.

I needed to get money somehow. Miguel's mother gave us a roof over our heads, and food. We needed food only when we weren't high. But money for heroin was a necessity, and as I wouldn't prostitute myself, I did what the male addicts in Spain did—became a blood donor. For half a litre of blood plasma, I was given a beer and a sandwich and money enough for two fixes. It was permitted to give blood every third day, except when you had a period. But as there were three private clinics in Barcelona which bought blood plasma and they had no mutual checking system, it was possible to go to one of them every day. And who would know when I had my period?

The clinics were amazing. Only outcasts and the very poor gave their blood there. They queued outside the closed roll-front long before the clinic opened. There were always more people wanting to give blood than there was room for. Inside the hall with the bunks, people smoked and sang, talking loudly as the nurses stuck needles into everyone's arms and ran back and forth with bags of blood. I attracted a certain amount of attention because of my Scandinavian appearance, but when they noticed that I didn't talk much they left me alone. Only once did I see another woman there.

Dependency would never have induced me to harm anyone else. I wasn't really like other addicts who suffered from a diminished control of their impulses. I hadn't got that. If I had had any impulses at all up till then, it had been more of a deliberate act to give way to them. An act that called for energy. No, I couldn't have knocked down or robbed anyone, and I never became one of those. I was a poor copy of an addict in that respect too, but more or less accepted despite everything.

Anyway, I now felt some impulses—of a sort, it seemed to me, that could drive me to destroy myself. In this way I came closer, via heroin—however absurd it may seem— to feeling like a real person. To have death as the stake seemed not unreasonable, when nothing else functioned. Having been unable to understand by achieving sameness, via comparing myself with others and recognising myself, I now seemed to be drawn to the absolute opposite, and this became a second opportunity to understand the same thing. I was not like the other addicts, and even when I did exactly the same things as they did, performed the same destructive actions, it was as if I smelt different. As if my scent said that I wasn't of the same sort, and as if that scent hung in the air around me. I was aware of it, but didn't know why it was so.

Life among the addicts had several advantages. There was a structure, there were rules for how to behave, and those rules were much clearer than in society outside. There was a solidarity, as well as an accepted subject of conversation—drugs. Everyone had the same main interest. The solidarity had clear limits, the same for us all when it came to the craving—everyone was for him or herself. There was just one thing you simply didn't do, a deadly sin, and that was you didn't squeal on anyone. If you squealed on someone, you had to reckon on it being picked up. A clearly obvious rule with a fixed punishment. You didn't cheat other addicts, either, even if you could cheat people in the society outside as much as you liked. But Miguel didn't stick too closely to that rule.

Among the addicts, there was a social clarity that it was a relief for me to have found. I could understand why people behaved in this way or that. Sometimes things were explained to me, at other times I worked them out for myself, but nothing seemed entirely incomprehensible. I was now also able to have some kind of relationship with a man, which made me feel more of a real person. To have a destructive relationship was at least more normal than having none at all. But all the time I was getting more and more ill and weak. I often fainted after giving blood. The climate was hotter than I was able to stand and the heroin made me swell up. In the end I became very ill. When I gave myself a fix, my temperature could swing between forty-two and thirty-seven degrees within half an hour. None of my internal organs seemed to be functioning. I hadn't eaten for a week and everything I drank I immediately threw up again. I realised I was dying. I could feel it in my body. But the death I had thrown in as a stake, the death I'd been prepared to pay with, had been a swift death. An overdose or an air bubble in the syringe that quickly went to the heart, or the strychnine it was rumoured someone who hated addicts mixed with the heroin. What I hadn't imagined was a slow, sick death. I was frightened. Something inside me woke up and said that's enough. I decided to stop.

It took time, but I went through with it. I probably suffered just as many withdrawal symptoms as other addicts did, but nonetheless I think it was easier for me to stop. I had an inner carrying-through mechanism that did what I had decided to do. It was a carrying-through mechanism that did not involve the emotions and refused to be distracted by impulses, a mechanism that could suffer anything. I had it for good or evil. It didn't evaluate the orders, just carried them out. If I looked into myself, I could feel just a little of that mechanism and then I knew I'd be able to do anything, anything I'd decided on. Once, the decision was made. Emotions and evaluation did play a part in the actual decision, of course, but then I simply carried out what I had made up my mind to do. My patience was infinite. If I had to wait, I could wait for any length of time, as long as was necessary. I didn't get impatient or irritated. I just did it, until it was done. And I did it all so thoroughly that I got past the ex-addict stage and went straight on to the level of non-addict. I was now free of the mental attraction to drugs which most people who have stopped using them have to live with for the rest of their lives.

2

Continuation

Sixteen

I was alone in Stockholm again and had no special desire to live. I felt empty, weary, exhausted, though I still didn't realise why. At the time, I didn't know that everything I did cost me a huge amount of energy. Like talking. To talk, I first had to think the words, almost write them in my head, usually twice if I was to say a longish sentence. Talking now went fairly quickly considering this long-winded process. I'd had my whole life to practise in and had become faster, but all the same it meant that I spoke more slowly than other people. This gave an apparent circumspection to my way of speaking, but most of all it robbed me of my energy.

The difficulty in linking thoughts and voice made it hard to keep up if more than two people were involved in a conversation. By the time I had thought out what I was going to say, and directed my voice to say it, the opportunity to say anything had usually passed. By then someone else had started talking, or even the subject had changed. As a result, I might either interrupt that person, or I would say nothing. I usually chose the latter. I never considered whether there might be another way of talking, or that other people perhaps didn't have to steer their speech manually. As long as my difficulties overloaded my everyday life, I hadn't time to analyse them.

Every time I had to cross a street where there were no traffic lights, I had to apply intense concentration in order to estimate how far away the cars were, and at what speed they were coming towards me. I would stand there for ages, to be quite sure there were no cars even at a distance.

If possible, I preferred to wait until someone else crossed the street, and I could rely on his or her judgement. In traffic, I didn't give a thought to having a handicap. Where would such a thought have found room when I was so busy getting across the street? I just felt vaguely different, and if I ever even touched on the thought of what I was really doing, it was only because I didn't want anyone to know how difficult I found it. I was ashamed that I couldn't even cross the street like an ordinary person, a real person.

I had now given up drugs, but I had no life. I felt a failure, and wondered whether it really was my own fault. I was aware that I wasn't well and needed help. The ramifications of the drugs business were so tangible—of course I had problems if I had been a heroin addict. And I so terribly wanted to understand myself and the world. I sought help in psychiatry and eventually, with a grant from the council, I started going to a private psychotherapist. I wanted to find out whether there *was* something wrong with me. But the therapist regarded this feeling of mine, this feeling of not being a real person, as a psychological expression of my belief that I had no rights. Because of my family history, she said, the right to feel myself a human being had been taken away from me. And this was the only reason.

Whatever problem I brought up, she supplied a number of psychological explanations. The fact that I always had to think before I spoke was probably due to my being afraid of saying the wrong thing. The fact that I couldn't shut out what people were talking about, that I got so exhausted in large places with a lot of people about and couldn't keep sounds away from me, was all probably due to my need to control everything around me. And that I needed to exert control was not strange, she thought, considering that I had been brought up in such a disturbed environment.

It all sounded logical. I bought the explanation, but

inside me, it didn't feel right. 'Perhaps,' I kept saying. 'I don't know,' I would respond even more often. 'Yes, could be,' I said sometimes, looking at the table on which lay the obligatory paper handkerchiefs. But I seldom had that sense of: Of course, that's it, that makes sense. It felt wrong, but I had never experienced what it was like to feel it was right, so what did I know? The paper handkerchiefs stayed there unused. What she said never aroused any feelings in me, apart from the confusion and sense of duality that she thought could be interpreted as angst, an angst which then naturally pointed to how difficult it was for me to talk about my family and childhood. I would never have imagined that apparently intellectual therapy was in itself capable of arousing angst, or that it was her way of interpreting my difficulties that made me feel ill from talking about them. I just trusted that she knew best.

The paper handkerchiefs remained unused and I made up my mind to use them, to cry just once to see if then I would feel more real; real people who went into therapy probably used those handkerchiefs. But it didn't feel anything special. And as this therapy wasn't about me but about the person I was trying to be in order to fit in, it was someone else sitting there crying to order.

Anyway, my therapist was the only person in the world who bothered about me, and this helped. I was quite alone and really did need someone to take an interest in me. I tried to trust her even when it felt wrong; she knew much more about people than I did. Also, I had been used for so long to the idea that everyone else was more right than I was, as well as the sense of my inner and outer realities not matching. The therapist was a trained psychoanalyst, and even though the treatment she was giving me was psychotherapy she thought I should try free association. I couldn't do that. And I didn't know why I just went silent and empty inside. 'It's angst,' the therapist said. 'Angst often feels like this.' Perhaps it did? What did I know? I knew only that everything turned silent and echo-ingly empty inside me when she asked me to free-associate.

'Say whatever occurs to you.'

Nothing occurred to me. I didn't know that my associations were so concrete that they could take only one well considered step at a time, if they moved at all. Nor did I know that for me it was quite impossible to combine free thinking with speech—whatever spontaneity there might be would be lost when I performed the very deliberate act of speaking. I became empty and silent, and I had to learn to regard this as angst. The psychotherapy became partly a course in finding suitable names for various states.

Many of the psychological models of explanation I had to choose from attracted me intellectually. They had a logic, and the therapist didn't really try to foist them on to me. 'Feel for yourself,' she said. 'You're the only one who can know. Only you can know what is true for you. Only you can know when it fits.'

She often repeated this, but I *didn't* know. I just had A and B to choose from, when C was in fact the answer. But how could I know? I felt nothing inside. Everything that was said became nothing but intellectual reasoning. It was my brain sitting there in the therapy chair and I was standing outside, not being let in. And sometimes, if I tried easing open the door to get at the real problem, it was as if I was invisible to the therapist, as if she didn't hear what I was saying.

When I described vague memories of not understanding the world around me and feeling that everyone else seemed to know something I didn't grasp, I was told that all younger siblings felt like this. And that in my family it certainly hadn't been easy to understand what was going on. Yes, that was true, I agreed with that. But ... There was always a 'but' inside me. But ... it wasn't enough. But ... there must be something more. But ... I didn't know.

I mostly felt respected in therapy, but I was occasionally offended. If I didn't feel emotions such as anger, irritation or envy, according to the therapist this meant that I had suppressed them because they were so heavily charged for me. I probably didn't dare be angry, she would say, because I was afraid of the extent of my anger if I let it out.

'But I don't feel any anger at all,' I said.

'No, exactly.'

So it was a sign of my fear of anger. The therapist always had an answer, and it was safe to be with someone who always had an answer.

I looked deep down inside myself—nothing. I found neither anger nor even a trace of suppressed anger. I explained to the therapist that I usually thought out when I should be angry, and decided with my intellect whether I had any reason to be upset about something, but that I could *feel* neither anger nor envy. Everyone had these feelings inside them, she said. That's what it was like, she knew. Everyone felt anger and envy. Except me, I wanted to say, but hardly dared. If I said anything along those lines, the therapist would tell me that I probably had some need to distance myself from the crowd, that it was probably a question of my not wanting to be like everyone else—I wanted to be special.

I was offended, but it was a long time before I dared say so. When I finally did, I was doubly offended because she considered that my feeling of offence actually had nothing to do with her. It was a memory of an earlier insult that I was now transferring to her. And in addition, my resistance to the idea that I had suppressed these emotions was evidence, in fact, that she was right. If I hadn't suppressed them, I would not have needed to be so offended by her having said that I had.

'I don't know,' I said, feeling confused. 'Perhaps it *is* so.'

But somewhere deep down, I knew she was wrong. I just didn't know in what way she was wrong. And even if what we were engaging in must look like an ordinary therapeutic process, even if she was certainly doing her job in the way she had been trained, it was only a semblance of therapy. I could see quite clearly what, according to her, it would be all right to talk about, and I adapted to it. I had to censor the rest. I continued in therapy, because I had a desperate need for help. I put my hopes in this turning out to be the right help, even if it didn't feel like it.

I was actually helped in various ways, the most fundamental probably lying in the fact that here was someone who was bothering about me. This meant that I began to care about myself and no longer continued in harmful and destructive situations. I needed someone who took an interest in me and at the same time would leave me in peace. All the explanations I was given on human behaviour also helped me to understand better how other people functioned, even if I couldn't get the explanations to fit me. The behaviour of others became less incomprehensible, which meant that I found it easier to be with people. But when I rid myself of my destructive behaviour, I didn't succeed in replacing it with anything else. There was just an empty space. I sat in that chair at the therapist's week in and week out, often in silence.

I was trying to be someone, but *I* didn't seem to exist among all the possibilities available, so it had to be someone else. I felt I was empty. I had peeled away the unafraid person, those individual characteristics, the special tastes I had had as a child. I hardly knew what I liked at all now. I didn't know if I was hungry or satisfied. I didn't know what kind of music I liked, or whether I liked music at all. I didn't know whether I liked the books I was reading or whether I just read them anyway. I didn't know if I preferred doing one thing or another. I didn't know if I was tired or not, whether I was cold or whether I was bored.

I tried imitating other people. Now that I was with people more, I had to be someone. People asked me what I wanted, what I thought. I took features from people I met and added them to me. I often took features from people who seemed very self-confident. I did this immensely skilfully. I became a chameleon—if I adopted Karin's way of sighing as she spoke, I could use it with everyone except Karin, and if I adopted Maria's taste in music, then I didn't talk about music with Maria. I was an empty jar that could be filled with anything. People's behaviour simply fell into the jar and I used it to try to feel myself someone, like a real person. I developed this strategy in order to be able to relate to people. If you were no one, you couldn't relate—you had to be someone. The people I met didn't know each other, and I met them separately as I had such difficulty mixing in groups. This was also a prerequisite for my theft of personality features to be able to function.

Another thing that made being with people more difficult was that I found it so hard to mix *and* do other things at the same time. If I was to converse, it required so much energy that I had to sit still at a table and concentrate on nothing else. The conversation included not only linking of thoughts, but also calculating when I should speak, when the other person would speak, and when I should speak again. I had actively to reinterpret what I heard so that I understood it and wouldn't appear slow. I had to recognise each time that 'I'd like that glass' meant 'Give me that glass', and the trouble was that hearing 'I'd like . . .' a great many times was no help, because I still had to sort it out each time—this means that, and with that is meant this, and so on. It was strange that all ways of being polite entailed saying something other than what you actually meant.

This ceaseless thinking and interpreting I could cope with at the same time as conversing with someone. If I was quite fresh, I could also manage being out amongst people and use part of my mind's capacity for sifting out disturbing sounds. But I simply couldn't do anything more complicated while also speaking. If I moved at the same time, it became altogether too much. I couldn't walk while talking, because I couldn't walk automatically—I had to think about walking to be able to do it. It was also very exhausting to stand for any length of time, although it could be easier to talk while standing. It was as if the force of thinking kept my body upright, as I actively had to think through the standing in order not to collapse. But I didn't know that then. It had always been like that and I had nothing to compare it with. I just thought I was lazy. I must be lazy and sluggish if I hadn't the energy to stand for the same length of time as others did.

These things made being with people even more difficult. It might have been easier to do things together with people, as just having relations with them was so complicated. But it just wasn't like that, because the doing simply couldn't be combined with mixing. Nor could I share other people's leisure interests, as they were often physically far too complicated. I couldn't ski or skate. I had no ball sense whatever. And I was terrified of landing in a situation where everyone was suddenly to play some ball game I couldn't manage. There was always so much I couldn't do, always so many limitations.

People sometimes tried to persuade me to join in, and I felt stupid when I didn't want to and couldn't explain why. But it was also often the wisest course not to allow myself to be persuaded. It could have been fatal not to know where the parts of my body were, not to be able to judge speed and distance, or to lose all sense of up and down on a ski slope.

I had quite a clear idea of what I could cope with and

what not, although I didn't know why it was so. Not daring to try things, I was sometimes considered cowardly, and I thought they were probably right. All physical activities were difficult, with the poor grasp I had of my body. But there were also other problems to do with moving—I couldn't perspire. However hot it was or however much effort I made, I never sweated, or no more than a little under my arms, anyway. Instead, I seemed to get hotter and hotter inside, with a heat that couldn't escape anywhere, a hot pressure increasing from within with all exits closed. This made taking any exercise a torment, but I did try to make myself, all the same. I had all my self-discipline and my inner carrying-out mechanism to call on. And still I thought that it was only my idleness impeding me, that all I had to do was simply make more of an effort.

I tried to be with people because I wanted to be a real person. I wanted to feel normal, but I actually felt very self-sufficient when alone. Wanting to share something with other people was more theoretical. Emotionally, I didn't suffer from spending time on my own. I painted a lot and I wanted to be an artist—a good profession for anyone wanting to be left alone. It was a way of legitimising my loneliness. I didn't miss other people, but I missed missing other people. I was trying to do something about it. It became a little easier to mix if I drank, so I drank quite a lot of wine, though not really much more than anyone else. It was just that the others had other relationships in their lives—parents, boy-friends, cousins, children, aunts—which didn't always involve drinking wine. I had none of those.

Seventeen

I was working at the day nursery again, and it seemed to me that I was liked there. My sense that rules were for obeying was well suited to working life. I was always on time, I never overslept, and I always did what I was supposed to do. They could rely on me. In some respects I was almost too good, as if I lacked the usual human failings. I suffered from some kind of exaggerated normality, which was the result of my lack of disturbing inner impulses and of my striving to be a real person. I was also appreciated for my work with the children. There was nothing a child could do that would arouse my annoyance. I could stand any amount of whining, nagging and obstinacy and I was often the one to look after the children the others considered difficult.

There was one little girl there who was finding it hard to learn to speak. Nina was almost three, and all her words sounded the same. She would go up to an adult and tug at her clothing, point at a chair and try to say 'chair'. Then she would want the adult to say the word, then Nina would say it again; then she would want the exercise to be repeated, over and over. The staff found her very hard work, and said it was just compulsive, ceaseless repetition. There was no point in giving in to her, because she obviously could never have enough of it. They considered it impossible to do as she wished, because she never gave in. Nina would jump up and down in fury if the adult wanted to stop or change to another word. She whined or tugged at her clothing if whoever it was tried to distract her attention.

Nina wasn't one of my group, so I hadn't spent much time with her. But one day when everyone was out in the nursery courtyard, I heard some of the staff complaining about how hopelessly difficult the child was and that they couldn't cope any longer. They were tired of her—they had tried to invent things for her out in the yard, to get her to laugh and play with the other children, but nothing had worked. She was impossible to reason with, but simply repeated words. Even if they didn't say so, most of them thought Nina a dull child with little charm. I didn't want to listen to their complaints. I wasn't tired of Nina and it saddened me that she somehow exhausted the staff. I decided to take Nina with me and go inside.

My idea was no more educational than that I saw clearly that this repetition of words was very important to her, though I knew nothing about what lay behind it. But I very much wanted her to know I realised it was important to her. I had the time and patience to let her go on with it. I saw no parallels with myself as a child, but presumably it was my own experiences that led me to feel intuitively how important this was for her.

Once we were indoors, Nina went straight over and pointed out of the window at a car in the street, then said something that sounded like 'ter'.

'Car,' I said.

'Ter,' said Nina.

'Car,' I said.

And so on we went, over and over again. This was costing me nothing. I didn't think it difficult, nor did it try my patience. We just went on, first me, then Nina. 'Car'— 'Ter.' 'Car'—'Ter . . .'

After half an hour of this, I could just make out a c at the beginning of her word, and now it sounded like 'curr'. After an hour—and how many times had I now said 'car'—thousands?—Nina was able to say 'curr'. She smiled and was delighted with her 'curr'.

After we had repeated 'Car'—'Curr' for a while, she suddenly turned her head, pointed at the lamp and said 'Oab'. She was ready now for the next word. Then it dawned on me that this was not at all a matter of an *idée fixe*. Nina quite simply *needed* to do it a thousand times, while other children perhaps contented themselves with twenty. Also, she *knew* she needed it, and worked hard to get the adults to help her. Her need for repetition was not excessive, just greater than what most people's patience could stand.

In time it also turned out that it was perfectly easy to reason with Nina. She would come and take hold of me, wanting to be allowed to repeat words on some occasions when I had no time at all. It was quite easy to explain to her that I hadn't got time then, but after lunch we could spend some time on it. I was able to stop her after a while, too, without her being angry or miserable, as long as I explained why we had to stop and that we would go on later. Once she knew that someone could see and understand at least some of her need, she was able to reason and compromise. And, once she was understood, Nina also had enough energy left to produce a little charm.

My endless patience and my ability to put myself into the children's situation were what made me good with them. I had no training and no theoretical basis to go on. Whenever I felt that I really was helping, I also felt great satisfaction with my work, and it was with children like Nina that I functioned best, one at a time. But child care very rarely entails one child at a time, and a great many things in the day nursery caused me considerable problems. I put a lot of work not only into avoiding problems, but also into trying to hide my own difficulties.

The children's parents were one of these difficulties. They never seemed to me to be anything but empty faces merging together. I couldn't remember what their names were, or which parents were whose. There were far too many of them. The nursery's thirty children and ten staff were already too many for me, and I had no room for any more faces. So I had to avoid all situations that involved meeting parents. I couldn't get enmeshed in questions such as 'What have you been doing today?' To be able to say what that particular group had been doing that day, I then had desperately to remember which was this parent's child. I was very often unable to recognise them at all. So I had to develop strategies in order to deal with situations of this kind. I would have preferred to steer clear of parents altogether, but I couldn't do that. I tried to arrange my working hours so that I avoided them as much as possible, choosing mornings only, when parents came holding their children's hands, rather than later in the day. I didn't know why it was so exhausting dealing with parents, and I had no words to explain it. I was fully occupied trying to manage every minute of my life. I knew the nursery staff considered that I didn't take on all the responsibilities I ought to, such as contact with parents, but they thought I was so good with the children that it made up for any peculiarities I had.

The more confused my surroundings were, the harder it was for me to sort out my impressions, and that drained me. I began to feel I couldn't go on working full time, but in the eyes of society I was young and healthy and had no reason to work less than forty hours a week. As usual, I just thought I must be lazy. All the others said they too found the work tiring, so what had I got to complain about? I tried to reduce my hours by half and live on less money. All my strength was running out of me, and I had no energy left for anything outside work.

Even though it demanded so much energy of me, hearing everything and being unable to shut out sounds had its uses at the nursery. In a room where there were many children playing in different groups, I knew what everyone was doing even when I was really occupied with only one.

As nothing escaped me, I could hear a conflict as it arose and intervene at once. I could see if someone was about to fall, and I knew what was happening in the next room. In other words, I usually had an overall view. But keeping my system going despite this overloading demanded maximum concentration—in fact, demanded far more than I could actually muster. Sometimes I went to the cloakroom and tried to give my senses a rest, but this was rarely of any use. The question of why I was so exhausted remained unanswered.

I usually managed to keep some kind of balance. Only very rarely did I end up in a blank, detached state at work, and that was only for short spells and in the kind of situation where I knew someone else would take on the responsibility. If I was alone with the children, I kept going, although it sapped my resources to the limit.

I often chose to do the cooking at the nursery. The staff were supposed to share all the work, but whenever I had any choice, I worked in the kitchen. Keeping track of all the things that had to be done at once could be difficult. If this was to cook for so long, when did I have to put on the potatoes for both to be ready at the same time? Should I lay the tables before or after? When should I make the salad and how much did I need? At the same time, I had to occupy the two children I had with me in the kitchen. But what I gained was a relatively quiet occupation; and I could make a strict plan for everything and then stick to it without anyone else suddenly intervening or changing anything. Sometimes, if they were all going on an outing, I didn't have to have children in the kitchen at all. Being alone there cooking was like being given a present; also, I didn't have to go home and sleep immediately after work. That day, I might have the strength to do something else apart from work. And yet it was for the children I wanted to be there, particularly for those times when I could understand and help.

One day I was cooking in the kitchen when Tor suddenly came in in floods of tears. Tor was one of those secure and healthy children I didn't know at all well. I asked him what had happened.

'Don't want to tell,' he said.

I tried coaxing him a little to tell me why he was so wretched.

'No.'

Impasse. I went on coaxing, saying that people often felt better after telling someone why they were miserable.

'That's what all grown-ups say,' said Tor.

I suggested that was perhaps because they had lived longer and knew it was true. Perhaps that was why grown-ups always said it.

'But I know it's not true,' said Tor tearfully. 'I've tried and tried lots of times and I know it's no use.'

I pointed out that he hadn't tried with me, and that sometimes you had to try several grown-ups before you found someone who understood. But Tor said that that was what he was miserable about, things the grown-ups didn't understand—they just said 'Oh, that's nothing.' So there was no point in telling grown-ups, he knew that.

I had one more go: as he hadn't tried me, he couldn't be sure I wouldn't understand, I told him. I actually knew there were children in my group, I added, who thought I was better at understanding certain things than other grown-ups were. In the end, he told me. He had climbed up on the back of a sofa that had been pulled out into the middle of the playroom because someone was sweeping the floor. There were some younger children on the sofa, who told him he wasn't allowed to climb on it.

He knew he wasn't allowed to, but he took no notice of them because they were only silly little kids. If any grown-up had told him he would have got down, but he reckoned he didn't have to take any notice of them, you didn't have to obey little children. He went on climbing and told the kids to mind their own business. And they went on telling him he wasn't allowed to climb there. Then, quite suddenly, as he was hanging over the back of the sofa, a grown-up came up from behind and lifted him off without saying anything or giving him a warning of any sort. And Tor was frightened and terribly upset.

I recognised that sense of violation mixed with fright when something uncontrollable suddenly happens. I also recognised that it was just the kind of thing adults thought unimportant. I was pleased I'd actually understood him and I could show him he was right, that lots of grown-ups say 'Oh, that's nothing' about things like that—probably because they've forgotten what it's like to be a child. It was precisely so that I could talk to Tor in the kitchen about such things that I wanted to work at the nursery. I didn't want to work there just in order to sort out provisions, draw up timetables, see to the organising and other such jobs I had a talent for and fled to when the impressions got too much for my nerves. That wasn't at all as nice as being with the children.

I felt bad about avoiding the children in so many situations when, despite everything, it was with them I wanted to work. I couldn't explain to myself why it was so. It also felt bad knowing that although the other staff appreciated me for what I was good at, they thought I didn't take full responsibility and considered me inadequate. I never became one of them. I always found myself on the sidelines. I never really counted.

Outings with the children were very hard work for me, and if I had the chance to stay behind at the nursery when the others went off, I often took it. Keeping track of a lot of children in new environments took far too great an effort. And yet I managed when I had to, by dint of total concentration and much inner activity. But still I couldn't understand why I hadn't the energy, why I was becoming more and more unhappy and exhausted. I liked the work, didn't I? And the staff liked me well enough. My status was quite good and they often asked my opinion, because I was a good observer. I would notice details the others might have overlooked and they were pleased to listen to me, for everything I said had been thoroughly thought through and I never rushed things. As I never became emotionally involved in anything, they often turned to me for mediation. I had no need for prestige, nor had I any competitive instinct, any pride to lose. I got on with everyone. Most of the children also liked me very much although, being predictable and always the same, I perhaps did not respond to the need that healthy children have for excitement.

Yet I couldn't cope with it. It was inexplicable, as if work was devouring me despite the fact that it was the first thing in my whole life I had ever thought I was good at. What was wrong with me, if I couldn't manage the simplest thing, couldn't keep a job I enjoyed? And if I couldn't live for my work and didn't have any life outside work, what then would I live for? I wanted to cope, but that wasn't enough. Why was I so lazy? Why, although I believed this was what I wanted, was I so stupid and disinclined? Why couldn't I just have a perfectly ordinary life?

Eighteen

After a few empty and drug-free years when I did nothing but work, I met Dirk. He chose me, and I allowed myself to be chosen. This was quite in line with the contradictions I had learnt life should contain. I liked him *and* disliked him, so everything was in order, just as it should be. The two contradictory truths constituted reality.

Dirk came from Belgium, but had lived in Sweden for a long time. So . . . Belgian, and an economist by profession. I thought this must be less destructive than my previous choice of a Spaniard and heroin addict. He seemed to be more ordinary than previous men I had experienced, and this was what I wanted—the ordinary, the real. I wanted to have a relationship because this was one kind of measure of the normality I wanted to achieve. I wanted to live with someone both because I thought you should live as a couple and because I wanted a model, someone who knew what you should do. Someone I could conform to. Dirk was now to be my model. He was a real person and perhaps his realness might rub off on me in some way? Perhaps I could also be a real person if I adapted my life to his? I wasn't aware of my aims, but I just knew that I was fighting for a place in life, a place where I could be.

In the early stages of our relationship, things went quite well. As usual, I imitated others in order to feel I was someone, so that he would see me as someone. I sensed that Dirk liked the features I had adopted from other people. He didn't know he was having a relationship not with me, but with a woman I had invented. It couldn't work. How could it have done? The invented woman wasn't real. She was empty, and I who was playing her was not real, either. No one, not even I myself, had ever seen me as I really was.

Things got worse when more intimacy was called for. Imitation couldn't rise to it—I didn't know who I should be. I started screening myself off and didn't always answer when spoken to. Dirk became more and more annoyed. I didn't understand his irritation as I had never had that feeling myself. But his anger hurt me with its hard, sharp scornful remarks. And the more hurt I felt, the more silent I became. Dirk was annoyed when, as he put it, I disappeared into the wall. I just wasn't present, he said. And couldn't I at least answer when he spoke to me? But I couldn't always do that. I became more and more unsure and increasingly inclined to try to hide my difficulties. At the same time, Dirk turned colder, more malicious. My way of either evading or being unable to take things in appeared to rouse in him an urge to see how far he could go, to see how much I could take.

I was used to people saying they cared for me, then offending me. It had been like this all my life. I was puzzled why he was so nasty to me. If he didn't like me, he didn't have to be with me, did he? His desire to be malicious bewildered me. I had never felt that, either. Nor did I know exactly what it was I was being exposed to, so I put up with a great deal. Furthermore, I wanted to understand what I didn't understand, and this made me continue with the relationship. I found it difficult to believe I was right to feel insulted when I didn't understand when he snapped at me. I tried to calculate with my intellect just when I ought to be angry, or just what I ought to feel.

Dirk complained that I always walked a step behind him and always did what he did. This was true. He was my model. I went where he went, ate what he ate, did what he did, hoping I would be a little more of a person, a little more real. I tried to put up with what was difficult for me, but I needed someone's help. I couldn't manage on my own, and Dirk was the only person there. I needed someone who could show me what you had to do to live. I needed a life. But Dirk restricted my living space more and more. He became increasingly malicious, while I held on to him to stop him disappearing. I thought that if I had a relationship, if I could say 'This is my boy-friend', then I was a more real person.

My way of taking what people said quite literally continued to lead to a great many misunderstandings. When Dirk saw my need for him to express himself clearly, so that I understood, he would talk even more obscurely. When he saw my need to know and to grasp how things were, he said it was none of my business. He often lied about all kinds of things, often about things that were totally unimportant, and this confused me greatly. He would laugh in a superior way or snap at my inability to cross the road, or at the fact that I had to plan everything I undertook so thoroughly.

Increasingly often I would find out that he had lied about something, but I could not understand why he did it. There didn't appear to be the slightest reason. I just grew more miserable and confused. I felt like no one at all. I mostly stayed with Dirk because I thought it was as he said, that I misunderstood him, that I misinterpreted, and that I only wanted to control him. I was so used to other people being right.

I couldn't manage the job and I had failed in a relationship. I left Dirk feeling a total failure, and with that ever-present, vague feeling that there was something wrong with me. I read books on psychology and tried to understand. Somewhere or other I must recognise myself. I certainly did occasionally, a little bit here and little bit there. But more frequently I recognised people around me in what I read. I tried everything—serious psychological works, Christian books, everything I could lay my hands on. I read anything that might possibly provide an answer.

One book I read was called *Understanding Your Loneliness*. On the back it said 'This book should be read by all those who think that no words or actions could ever save them from the torment of their own loneliness.' I read a great many wise words about many kinds of loneliness in that book, but arrived at the last page without having got anywhere near my kind of loneliness. I tried everywhere. I was the little girl at the day nursery who found it difficult to learn to speak. So I tugged at whoever and whatever came my way to see if they could help me.

The therapist I had gone to had regarded my searching, whatever it was that drove me on, as a way of being hard on myself. She thought I should learn to be nice to myself. But my subconscious seemed to know that help would never reach me if I sat myself down and was nice to myself. I had to whip my nervous system a little to keep it going. I also had to find time to understand everything that was so obscurely strange about me before it was too late, before I lost all desire to do so and took my own life.

I read various medical books and decided I must be a hypochondriac, because sometimes I thought I recognised myself in such different illnesses and handicaps. But I didn't really believe I had those illnesses—there was always far too much that didn't fit. All the same, such things interested me and I pushed on. I wanted to know, wanted to understand. But there was no book that answered the particular questions I wanted to ask, and I didn't even know how to put the questions. I took out all the books the library had on innate abnormalities, because I kept telling myself this was what I was interested in. They were very old books with words such as 'abnormality' and 'malformation'. I wasn't really aware that I was looking for myself and I certainly couldn't find myself among those abnormalities, although I thought I had one or two physical signs in common with the retarded.

I did have a kind of engine now, which ran on my life-long desire to understand, but I didn't always generate enough energy to keep going. Then I would lose speed, slide back into myself or just become wretched and tired, not wanting to live any more. I also tried working at understanding others. I listened to the way they talked and tried to learn their empty chatter. It was uphill work. I thought hard about it and trained myself at what one should say and when. I studied people, and usually spoke only when I had something to say. I couldn't understand talking for the sake of talking. It seemed superficial and stupid. But when I looked at people, I began to have some inkling that there were other things going on under the surface, that chat wasn't just chat. I always approached whatever I undertook seriously—I was unable to take any other attitude. But psychotherapy had made me reflect more on what I was like, and my wish for a more easy-going and spontaneous side of me grew stronger. I somehow felt that I probably did have a side of that kind. If only I didn't have to use all my strength to get me through everyday life, if only I could understand and be understood, then I would have a little strength left over.

I wanted to study. If my poor marks at school had been due to my laziness, I thought, or if I hadn't been able to cope with school because of the family, as my therapist had said, then things should go better now. Moreover, as I couldn't cope with the job, I had every reason to try something else. I started reading university entrance subjects at adult education classes. As I could choose in what order I took the subjects, I started with languages, as I found them easiest. At first I got top marks in everything. I did a three-year Spanish course in one term. I started recouping a little of the self-confidence I had lost with Dirk. But after a term or two, I had to take other subjects as well, and this proved more difficult. All the same, I often succeeded in compensating for what I found difficult in a subject by being good at something else in it—by doing a special project or something similar—with the result that I gained at least reasonable marks. The teachers saw that I was ambitious, although they couldn't make out why I achieved such poor results in certain areas.

I had no difficulty learning facts, and would have perhaps done better at a school of the old type, where you learnt dates and events, births and deaths of kings by heart. But in modern history tests you had to account for the connections—how and why did this happen? Which factors were important to the course of this war?

I sat at home with my books, trying to see the connections, but it was hard. Every little bit of fact seemed to land in its own compartment in my head and refused to be linked with any other. I tried poking into details. I dissected them and hoped a unified whole would appear, but it rarely did. I would almost have preferred to be lazy, because the familiar old image of myself as lazy and stupid seemed easier to bear than the feeling of endlessly trying and still not being capable. In the sciences, I managed to compensate for the incomprehensibles of chemistry by knowing all the eras of the earth and the names of all the species of rock. I already knew how the human body functioned: that wasn't difficult—after all, I had read so many medical books. But after the major science test, the teacher thought it strange that I hadn't succeeded in getting one single answer right in the chemistry section, when all the other answers had been correct. She wanted to give me a good mark. 'Was it a momentary lapse?', she asked me. Couldn't I just repeat that section with another class she took? So that she could give me a higher mark in the whole subject? I couldn't explain why I had failed the chemistry and I agreed to re-sit the subject. I worked away at it, staring for hours at the books and trying to learn, but I couldn't take it in and the little I did drum into my head didn't stay there. I re-sat the test and failed again. I didn't know why. When it hadn't worked however much I'd tried, I felt a complete failure. With my being so ambitious in the other science sections, the teacher was sorry she couldn't give me a better mark.

When I gave up the classes, I had fought my way to high marks in many subjects, but all the same I had no leaving certificate. There was one subject that had been impossible—maths. There was no area in maths that I could compensate with. I was still simply incapable of thinking in the way maths demanded, and it had turned out to be utterly beyond me. I couldn't even do the simplest things. If kilometres, miles and litres were included in the same sentence, I couldn't keep them apart. They just floated together. How many kilometres to a mile? I didn't know. I couldn't know, if at the same time I had to think out something else. I didn't understand what I was reading. The words and symbols were like a tangle of rubber bands that I had to sort out. As soon as I got hold of one band, I lost the first one I'd been holding, and with a snap it whizzed back into the tangle again. At worst, by then it had become even more enmeshed, and at best I had to start all over again from the beginning.

When I was sitting there with a page of questions in front of me with someone explaining, I could understand that I was to divide the first number by the second, but I had no idea *why* I should do that. So I never knew how to recognise a calculation of that kind, either, should I have come across it somewhere else. I was also totally hopeless if the question was put in another way. Whatever I did, it didn't help. I had no strategies at my disposal, and so it was quite impossible. And with no maths, no leaving certificate. I had failed again.

I started working at the day nursery again. But I still hadn't the strength required for this kind of job. I couldn't sort out the disorder of my surroundings, and my persistent efforts despite this to do a good job seemed to consume my energy and chew away at my nerve ends. There grew less and less of me. I was ebbing away. My life-long need to be always prepared for things was also eating away at my strength. I had to be mentally prepared for every step I took. The thought always had to be a step ahead of the action. It was habit to function like that, and it didn't really do me any harm—indeed, in a way I liked being like this. It was me. But I still didn't know why I was more exhausted than the others, or why a forty-hour working week might in practice entail eighty for me.

I had no stress tolerance. In two seconds, stress could consume all the energy I needed to get through a whole day. So I had to adapt my life to accommodate any eventuality. Under no circumstances should I risk exposing myself to pressure. I lived constantly on the very edge of what I could cope with. I was always using up my reserves. This meant that my need for sleep was utterly inflexible, for if I went short in that area there was nothing to top it up with. I had to have my eight hours. Otherwise, I couldn't find the energy to steer manually the person who was me, manoeuvring the forces necessary to enable me to think all the time all the things I had to think in order to be able to do anything at all. If I couldn't follow each action in my mind, it would not be carried out, or else I wouldn't be able to find my way back to a certain moment in my memory. I wouldn't know where I had put something down or what I had just said.

Following the trail in my mind was absolutely necessary. It was like the breadcrumbs that Hansel dropped behind him in the fairy-tale when he and Gretel were taken into the forest. I marked out tracks in my mind so as to be able to find my way back. Preferably, if there was time and place in my mind, I needed to double-check the thought or action, imposing a slight delay so that I would know where I really had put that thing or what I had just done. Like turning the crumbs into stone so that the birds wouldn't eat them. I had done this all my life, and I never considered that there could be any other way, or that this was why my strength seemed to keep leaking away. With all those voices from childhood now incorporated in my ego, I simply said to myself, 'You can if you really want to! Wake up! Pull yourself together! You're just lazy.' But that was hardly any use at all. I just grew more and more wretched and weary. It felt as if the amount of energy I had been allocated and that was meant to last for eighty years was running out. As if you were born with a lifetime's energy and I had already used mine by the time I was twenty-five. My need to reduce everything to one person at a time and one thing at a time simply expanded. I could no longer stay at the nursery.

What should I do? I tried studying again, Spanish at the university this time. I didn't really know what use it would be, but I was good at languages. If I couldn't hold down a job I had to do something else, and there wasn't much to choose from. I also wanted to find out whether I could cope with university. I had to know whether I was stupid or lazy or backward, or just odd. Although I hadn't the relevant certificate I was able to get into university all the same, because there was a rule that said you could enter if you were twenty-five and had been in employment for at least four years.

First, I took a compulsory course in general Spanish grammar and phonetics. The course was really based on lectures, but since I found verbal information difficult to take in I read books with a lot of numbered paragraphs. This was just the kind of thing I liked and that stuck in my mind. At the exam, I just turned to the right page in my head and read what was there. It was easy. My self-confidence increased, and I also managed certain parts of the main course with no problems. Spanish grammar and pronunciation went well, but things took a turn for the worse when we had to learn the history of Spain and Latin America.

The teaching was all in Spanish, so I had a good head-start in the language over my fellow-students, many of whom had come straight from school. And I had lived in Spain—true, among bank robbers, drug addicts and prostitutes—so I was used to hearing spoken Spanish and at speed. Yet it didn't go well. I couldn't get the individual bits of history to cohere into a whole. I could only see them separately, which meant that I could never take in the contemporaneousness of history.

However, at the end of term I had passed in all parts and gained the right number of points. But I reckoned I had been awarded the requisite number out of benevolence, and my instinct told me I would never reach the full forty points I had ultimately to get. Material provided only verbally at lectures and that couldn't be read somewhere posed a problem for me, as I needed a written basis in order to be able to study. I wouldn't be able to compensate for this in the long run. I had my twenty points and that looked good. But in fact, I had failed yet again.

I saw no other options, so once again I went back to working at the day nursery. I had been on leave of absence, so all I had to do was to go back and start work. I really wanted to cope now, so why shouldn't I? But the days at the nursery became a long series of preparations, fending off, avoiding, and an endless sorting-out of impressions. They called for intense concentration, and I was having constantly to direct myself seconds before the curtain went up. When my strength gave out, I changed jobs. I started working with old people instead, with handicapped people and some with senile dementia. This was much duller, but the surroundings were better, quieter and calmer. The tempo of the pensioners was like balm to my nerves. I usually had to work with one person at a time, and this suited me. By working evenings and nights, I could also earn a salary I could live off without having to work full-time.

My concrete way of understanding suited the senile well. They might seem very confused, but I discovered that in many of them there was something logical and absolute in their way of expressing themselves. Elsa was one of these. She was a woman with senile dementia who had recently come into sheltered housing. She often used to say 'I want—I want—I want', as if addressing the air. She sometimes grabbed people and kept repeating the same words. She would usually get hold of newcomers and try to hang on to them while repeating her 'I want—I want—I want.' This was just the way Elsa was, I was told. When I asked what it was she wanted, the others working there told me there was no point in asking her—she would just go on and on in that way. It was better to talk about something else and try to break the repetition. I did as they said, but after a while I noticed she always patted her chest three times whenever she said 'I want.' The staff frequently used this as a reason to try to stop the repetition and instead start talking about her necklace, which she often wanted to show you anyway. On these occasions she might grow angry, thumping her chest more persistently, and when the staff tried to divert her fury and stop her from harming herself she grew angrier than ever.

One evening when the staff had gone home and I was alone with them all, Elsa took hold of me.

'I want,' she said crossly, and thumped her chest.

As I thought so concretely, I asked her, despite what the others had said, what she wanted. Then we sat there for quite a long while.

'I want—'

'What do you want, Elsa?'

'I want.'

She thumped her chest. Thump—thump—thump.

'What do you want?'

'I want!'

It was nothing to me to go on for ever. I didn't even think about it. My patience meant I just continued. After a long spell of repeating the words, Elsa made a different gesture and I suddenly realised what she wanted.

Instead of patting her chest, she cupped her hand and drew a breast in the air. Then I knew what she had meant by the chest-thumping.

'Milk! Is it milk you want, Elsa?'

'Yeeees,' she said, as if the word was one long sigh.

After that, it turned out that it was milk she wanted every time when she said 'I want—I want—I want.' One of her relatives later confirmed that Elsa had always drunk a lot of milk before she had moved into the home. But the old people weren't given milk there. It had been taken for granted they wouldn't want it. I was able to recognise myself in Elsa. I knew what it felt like not to be understood, and it pleased me that I could help her.

But although this job did not entail the same exhausting disarray as the day nursery had, and although in some ways it was better for me, it was a poor compromise. I was pleased to be able to help and I liked using what talent I had, but I was mostly unable to do anything for anyone. There was no life in the old people, at least very very seldom. Depression, pain and death reigned there. A large part of the work was dealing with their anguish and their excrement. I didn't think much of that. I didn't like the work, but it was a price I thought I had to pay.

I had liked the day nursery but hadn't managed to cope with it. This work I managed to cope with, but I didn't like it. I noticed that many of the others who worked there had lives full of interests outside their work, and I hadn't. I didn't realise that you had to be fit and satisfied with

231

life to be able to manage a job that gave so little back. As I was good at the job, I thought, I had to do it, regardless of whether I liked it or not. I had to be grateful to have a job that didn't take up all my energies. Trying to get work that would give me something in exchange seemed impossible. I slogged on.

I was not really suited to irregular night work. I needed routine and proper sleep. At the same time, the night was the calmest period in the twenty-four hours, when there was plenty of time to prepare myself for everything I had to do. Night work also brought with it more free time to gather my strength. On the one hand and on the other . . . in the end, every compromise became untenable. In the end, failure was always waiting. It didn't work, not this time, either. My energy was insufficient. Why was I so lazy and stupid and why couldn't I manage the simplest things? Why wasn't I a real person? And if I *was* one, why in that case did I think I wasn't? Why couldn't I simply pull myself together?

I sank to the very bottom of the depression I had lived with since I was ten years old. Down there it was very dark, an eternal black bog with no horizons. Now and again a thunderstorm rumbled past down there at the bottom of the pit, lightning flashes of mental pain struck me, burnt into my soul and left the dull taste of having struggled this far all for nothing. Because it was all to come to an end now. I looked around down there and it was empty. I had no family, no job I liked, no one close to me. Nothing. I was unable to mobilise the will to act, not even to take my own life. I just wanted to lie down and die. My energy had finally expired. I had used up everything and there was nothing left inside me, nothing but a vague sense of humiliation at having been deceived into continuing this far. Deceived by the vain hope of becoming a real person.

Nineteen

It now dawned on me that my whole life had been a pretence. Everything had amounted to trying to be someone else and hiding my difficulties so that no one would see them. Nothing had been real. I was terribly lonely, and not until then had it really sunk in that I had never been close to anyone, and that something quite essential separated me from the rest. I hadn't even wanted to be close to anyone else, not with my feelings, anyway. I had just wanted, as an idea, to be close to someone. Because it should be like that in order to be a real person. I and my whole life were nothing but a contrivance, and it seemed unspeakably meaningless. I fell and fell until I hit the bottom of the pit.

I tried desperately to get help. I didn't know where that help might be found, but I started again with my therapist. When I talked to her about my loneliness, she talked to me about the incurable loneliness of the soul. We were all lonely within ourselves, she said. But I felt stronger now in my grief. I had nothing to lose. I had the courage to tell her that I didn't think she was listening to me, that I felt violated by her way of interpreting what I said. She said I only saw it *as if* she was violating me, but it wasn't at all the case. It was only my past that made me now feel offended. I was confused again and not helped by what she said, but I knew of no other way. Though it seemed a hopeless task, I was trying to save my life. As always, I went on reading a great deal. I was on sick-leave now and really did have time to read.

My driving force to understand people, to understand

myself, attracted me to two library shelves: V, medicine and psychiatry, and D, psychology, I went systematically through them and borrowed and read whatever seemed interesting. I didn't think I was looking for anything special. And when I took out a book on autism and autism-related states, I didn't think anything of it. I just thought that here was yet another thing that might be interesting to read about. But suddenly I had turned the right page in the right book. I recognised myself.

There was far too much of me described for it to be sheer chance. I tried to talk to my therapist about what I had read, but she thought it destructive to entertain the idea that there was anything wrong with me. She maintained that it was my surroundings that had made me feel that. And when she saw that I didn't really accept her explanation, she added that diagnoses of this kind were used in a destructive way: it was said that the patient had brain damage, and people were not helped by being told that damage to their heads was to blame for whatever they thought was wrong with them. I didn't know what to believe. I tried to use my intellect and think out how things really were. I wanted to believe the therapist—that was the simplest. After all, if she was right, then I was sitting exactly where I should be, and at that very moment getting the help I needed. I really did want her to be right. But what I had read in the book, and recognised myself in, had hit me straight in the solar plexus. It was not just an intellectual explanation with which to satisfy the mind. At the same time, there were some things in the book on autism that didn't match the way I was, and I realised that if I suffered from anything like it, then it must anyway be a mild form.

I couldn't be satisfied with my therapist's assurance that there was nothing wrong with me, that it was just the misery I had grown up in that made me think that. I had to search further—here, perhaps, was a means of understanding myself. I tried to get the therapist to listen to what I was saying, at the same time looking for people who could help me get to the bottom of it. Could it be that in some way I was slightly autistic? But the therapist did not want to listen. She supported me, she said, but she didn't want to listen or learn anything new. She already knew what she needed to know about autism, and on the whole she did not believe it was a handicap with biological causes. She made it quite clear to me that nothing I said would make her change her opinion, for she had, as she said, met people who had dared stop being autistic. She believed it was a question of courage. I desperately tried to get her to listen to me, and explained that it didn't feel as if she was hearing what I said, that it didn't feel as if she respected me. But she turned it back on to me.

'And what does that remind you of? Was there anyone close to you when you were a child who you considered didn't listen to you?'

'Yes, everyone.'

'Then you're probably now confusing me with one of them, but I certainly do listen to you. I respect your view. But perhaps you find it difficult that we sometimes disagree?'

What could I say? I had never in my whole life found it difficult to accept that people had different opinions from mine. I'd been coming to her for four years and she hadn't even noticed it. But if I said this to her, she would in all certainty say that it could be that I was not aware of feeling like this. I left the therapist with a heavy sense of disappointment. I had put so many of my hopes in her and it hurt that she didn't even understand why I put an end to it.

Now I was hunting for someone who might help me understand, and the doctor I finally found worked in Göteborg. He was the first who didn't have that 'There's nothing whatsoever wrong with you, my dear little lady' attitude. And although on my first visit he said that I didn't give an impression of autism, I felt noticed and respected. I also knew that I could hardly be *severely* autistic. So I travelled to and from Göteborg a few times and had neuro-psychological tests, both there and in Stockholm. At last I had come to a place where I was taken seriously and where they knew a lot about my kind of difficulties. In addition, I read a lot more about autism and similar handi-caps, and for the next six months or so that the investi-gation took I came to understand a number of things about myself.

I started writing down what I found out. Eighteen months before I'd happened to read that first book on autistic handicaps, I had been off sick with depression. That was the first time in my life when I hadn't actually felt totally overburdened. Up till then, it had taken all my strength to get through everyday life. For the first time, I had energy left over to look at myself properly. I dis-covered that it couldn't be normal to be constantly exhaus-ted, to be always living on the edge of what I could cope with. Being off sick was a prerequisite for me to be able to go through the self-therapy that writing things down entailed.

I had recently met Kerstin again, and we were trying to get to know each other. Kerstin had lived in Sweden for many years now, and we had occasionally made unsuccess-ful attempts to make contact with each other. She said it was the first time she had felt she could communicate with me. And something had actually happened in me that made it possible for me to now speak automatically. I had never been able to do this before. I no longer had to think out everything I wanted to say, and I didn't have to direct my voice to say what I wanted said. It was pleasing that it worked all by itself. But it also saddened me to realise that it had always been this easy for other people, that they had never had to think about it, that it just came to them free. I wished someone had been able to explain this to me when it was still so difficult. I could have done with a little appreciation for actually succeeding so well despite my difficulties. Now I had to give myself that appreciation in arrears. And in a way, it seemed too late.

I couldn't say how it had happened—how it was that I could suddenly speak automatically. I don't suppose it really happened all that suddenly, but that's what it seemed like when I thought about it. Perhaps it simply got successively better and better without my really noticing it. Maybe for a long time I did it in the old way, thinking and writing in my head, because I was so used to it, even after I was able to speak spontaneously. Anyway, it seemed as if the last stage, when I no longer had to put any energy at all into my speech, only took a month or two. I could now also explain what I thought or felt in quite a different way from before. I found I could ask about things, too. I hadn't done this before—I'd always tried to think things out for myself. I talked to Kerstin about all this and she said it was good at last to know what she had intuitively known as a child—that her sister was not like other children. She also read the book on autistic handicaps and said that it should be called 'The Explanation of My Younger Sister'.

I went to Göteborg and the doctor talked about ADD and about Asperger syndrome—he said that as a child I might have been diagnosed as having Asperger syndrome. Between visits to the doctor I read a lot, and soon considered myself my own expert. The self-diagnosis I made was ADD with autistic features, and although I noted that there were many difficulties linked with ADD that I did not have, I felt satisfied with the diagnosis I had come up with and thought I could live with it—that I had ADD with autistic features. In Göteborg I also did parts of an intelligence test called WAIS. Afterwards, the doctor gave me what I took to be his final diagnosis.

'It can be confirmed that you have something within the spectrum of autism,' he said.

This didn't sound too bad. As far as I was concerned, I could bear that diagnosis, too. It felt true, and I could see myself in those words. So I went home with that label, which some people thought useless and destructive, but which I believed would help me. When I got home, though, I was terribly unhappy. I felt ill, damaged, disturbed. I didn't really know what was me or features of my personality, and what I should regard as a handicap. I thought perhaps the therapist had been right, that this kind of diagnosis was destructive. After all, look how ill I was feeling now. In wanting to find out how things actually were, I seemed to have generated my own difficulties. As if, just as everyone had always said, it was all my own fault. I had myself to blame for being so miserable. But I also felt incredibly relieved at having had what I had known confirmed. Yet desperately abandoned as well. It was so confusing. Why was there no one to ask me if I needed anything, whether I could do with some help? Not that I knew what I would have said in reply, but I did wish someone had asked.

I was miserable, but at the same time I had acquired a great many insights into how things all hung together, how I functioned and why. This meant that parts of my life became easier to deal with. I didn't want those insights, but neither did I want to be without them. They were a sorrow and at the same time a redress. A relief, but at the same time a pain. And I simply couldn't measure this confirmation of my handicap in terms of good or bad, although I did try.

A few days after that last visit to the doctor in Göteborg, I received a copy of a letter that he had written. It was a letter I had asked him to write and I'd been pleased when he offered to send me a copy. I thought it would be good to know what was in it, and I really had appreciated the fact that I had been met with honesty and straightforwardness in Göteborg. But when I read the letter, it saddened me. It began with the words, 'Gunilla Gerland is a woman with high-functioning autism . . .' I wasn't that! I hadn't agreed to be called that! The letter couldn't be about me. I couldn't see myself in those words—'high-functioning autism'. It wasn't something I could say about myself. Gunilla Gerland simply didn't fit with the words 'high-functioning autism'. They couldn't be put in the same sentence.

The strange thing was that I actually thought the 'high-functioning' was worse than the word 'autism'. High-functioning. Somehow, it sounded so degrading. Like something you might say about an object that was slightly defective—'. . . it's high-functioning, nevertheless.' Or like the breezy assertion, 'It tastes just as good, all the same', when a sponge cake comes out absolutely flat. And anyway, I didn't think I was even truly autistic, so how could I be a woman with high-functioning autism?

But after a while these words were no longer so important. Perhaps they needed to be digested, and then I would feel that what I called myself was what counted? Anyway, I was less wretched, and I still had access to that self-consoling unit within me. Though the value of self-consolation had fallen, and it no longer felt so good to turn inwards on myself for solace. Now I knew that, and I also knew why you should turn to other people for it. And I *wanted* to want to turn to other people.

3

Now

Twenty

A great many of my difficulties now cause me much less trouble, though some remain unchanged. I no longer have problems crossing the street, and yet I still maintain a habitual caution in traffic because of my previous difficulties. I can now judge speeds and distances, and I presume the improvement in this is also the reason why I am less clumsy. I find it easier to sense the way my body relates to my surroundings. But all the same, I do wonder whether I don't still judge speed and distance in some kind of 'manual' way, because when I'm tired it can be more difficult.

On the whole, I still have an absolute need for adequate rest each night. I can't survive my kind of life if I haven't slept properly. An hour's sleep too little is almost disastrous. This means I always have to be strict with myself about what time I go to bed and, of course, this contributes to my general lack of spontaneity. Periodically, I find it hard work, because sleep is so sensitive to mental influences. I have found myself in an exhausting cycle in which I cannot get to sleep, and because I know I am so dependent on sleep to be able to function, it's difficult to relax. Otherwise, measured by autistic standards, I think I am very adaptable, although by ordinary standards my flexibility is poor. I need to be prepared for everything that may happen, and I find it very difficult if someone wants to change something at the last minute.

I still follow everything I do in my thoughts, although I have become so practised at it now that I can do it very quickly. But if I'm unprepared when faced with a new situation, it becomes difficult to deal with the newness at the same time as thinking out everything I'm doing. Thinking is necessary. It's the only way I have of finding my way back into my memory. If I didn't follow it all in my mind, I would never have the slightest idea where I had put my shoes, where I had left my handbag, where the lavatory is, or how I would find my way back from somewhere. Other people seem to have this kind of memory, good or bad, somewhere in them, as if they just know where they've put something without having to think about the fact of having put it there. What is paradoxical is that, lacking this kind of memory, I have much better control over where I am or where I have put something down than many other people have. As I follow it all so closely in my thoughts, I know exactly where I've put something and seldom forget anything. Also, I often automatically register where other people have put things so that I can tell them when they can't find them.

Another automatic feeling that is lacking in me—and this is something I find harder to live with—is my inability to sense what people want of me. I am unable to perceive whether people wish me well or ill. Instead, I try to calculate with my intellect, and the result is not always that good. I've realised that people can sense if someone wishes them well or ill. They seem to accumulate some kind of experience of others, which they then use in order to read them. I have no such sense, no special place in which to accumulate those experiences. When someone says something hurtful to me, I often simply react to the words themselves without really being able to weigh up whether that person likes me or not. This has led to a lot of misunderstandings. But now I have at least realised that it is not really reasonable to think that someone who I know likes me, but who arrives late for an appointment, for instance, is doing so just to insult me. Though it's still purely intellectual knowledge that I have to weigh up every time I need to decide about someone's intentions. It has been just as difficult to grasp that some people have actually wished me harm. When people behave provocatively, they usually say very concrete things and I tend just to focus on their words without reading the meaning behind them. This means that I'm not in the slightest provoked by things many people seem to explode over.

In my teens, when I encountered provocation far more frequently than now, I would listen to admiring words from other people on how splendidly I put people in their place. I accepted this flattery, but at the same time I was confused because I wasn't at all aware that I was putting whoever it happened to be in their place. I had simply replied quite precisely to what they had said. Similarly, if someone said 'How plain you are', then I would answer 'Do you think so?' or just 'Oh yes', quite unaffectedly. I wasn't at all hurt by someone I didn't know thinking I was plain. What they thought had nothing whatsoever to do with me, had it?

I have also seen children's provocative behaviour incensing adults, but it really has no effect on me if a child yells 'You're silly—I don't like you.' Others don't *have* to like me, and when it comes to children I'm able to like them anyway, regardless of what they think of me at a particular moment. I find it very difficult to understand, even endure, that grown adults can get so angry with children.

My way of functioning has also meant that occasionally I find it difficult to show understanding of other people. I can't help thinking that people are rather pathetic in their need to be loved by everyone; that they are naive not to be able to disregard their own feelings, to keep things and people apart, even. But usually I just feel sorry for them when they can't. And when they get embroiled in strange conflicts or can't reason clearly and factually, then I'd like to *be them* for them, so they didn't confuse the issue so. But now I've realised I needn't be sorry for them, because they do gain something from what seems so troublesome to me. They think it's good to get so involved, and that people really are concerned about others. They perhaps even want to be drawn into conflicts and then complain about it, because they think it's just part of life. They don't always mean what they say; they can say something is upsetting when in fact they like it.

I still occasionally misunderstand things people say to me, but I think this is happening less and less frequently. A typical incident of this kind is when an acquaintance said 'You can phone me at work', and I thought she didn't want me to phone her at home any longer. I took it to mean I simply wasn't to phone her at home. When the misunderstanding was cleared up, she explained to me how unreasonable it would be for her suddenly to say I couldn't phone her at home, after we had known each other for so long. I hadn't thought it unreasonable. I had simply taken in exactly what she had said, and hadn't heard the implied meaning, 'You can phone me at work as well if you like.' I thought 'can' was the same as 'shall' or 'are to', because that's what I'd learnt. So that's what I understood. I hardly dare think how many times mis-understandings of this kind have occurred over the years and have never been sorted out.

My inner 'reinterpretation mechanism' is what tells me what things mean. It takes much less time nowadays to deduce that 'Of course you'll get work' really means 'I hope you'll get work.' I've learnt that it doesn't mean that the person who says this in some mysterious way knows that I will get work, even though I myself don't know. And yet I have to think and reinterpret phrases every time I hear them.

Going to new places still isn't easy, but I can if I have to. It requires planning and thorough preparation. Going to a town I've never been to before can be like stepping into a minefield. I have no overall view of it. I have no idea how it's organised or structured. I don't know what *colour* it is. And I may feel I'd really rather stay at home—always. What makes it so complicated is that I really like travelling and going to places I've been to before, but it's that wretched first time that is so difficult.

I have always tried to hide how much I have to prepare myself on these occasions, because it has happened that people have laughed at all my planning. I've been to the library and studied maps, found out about buses and other things—nothing can be left to chance. I've thought out every detail a thousand times. All that remains, what I can't prepare for, is the town's tempo, what the air feels like, what the town sounds like—everything that gives it a colour inside me. I don't think people understand, not even when I tell them that by changing something they can ruin hours of planning and mental preparation. They say 'But surely it doesn't make any difference if you go on the 12th instead the 14th, or if you leave in the morning instead of the evening.' There *is* a difference.

It's usually easier if I have someone with me when I'm to do something for the first time. Then, in a way, I can rely on that person's nervous system. There have been times when I have almost used other people for that purpose. I've been able to pretend that I want their company, while in fact what I've needed is an escort. I've made sure of having someone with me to a museum or a gallery that I've never been to before, just in order to be able to go there on my own later, without any problems. I have occasionally wished that I could link up with someone else's nervous system, like a computer on a network, and use it in situations of this kind. Needing to have the other person with me and thus having to be sociable and do things at the same time is something I still find difficult. I need to sit down and just be with people when it's a question of socialising, because it requires so much energy.

I also still think a tremendous lot. This means that I must have a great deal of solitude and create time to think, since I cannot think at the same time as doing everyday things, when my thoughts are absorbed in keeping up with what I'm doing. I'm good at a lot of things, perhaps more than many other people. And as I haven't been used to turning to others for help, I've had to teach myself things I need to know. Consequently, I'm good at things I have some talent for as well as things not nearly so easy to learn. I'm good at cooking, cleaning and making clothes. But I'm also good at repainting and renovating furniture, and I can put electrical things together. I'm good at reading instructions, filling in forms and putting things down in writing. As a non-flexible person, I'm also versatile. I can draw and paint, and I'm good at sorting and organising, as well as operating a computer. Largely speaking, everything I can do I have taught myself—everything except taking the skins off potatoes.

I have observed other people and seen that they don't think they have to know everything, that they are fairly satisfied with being good at a few things and then asking others for help with things they can't do. I've realised that they often think it good if people can complement each other with what they can do. I have to agree that seems practical, but I'm not used to thinking like that, as I'm so used to managing on my own.

Observing what other people do has always been my way of trying to teach myself to be like them. But nowadays, I mostly use my powers of observation in order to understand what I have in common with others and what distinguishes me from them. I no longer imitate other people's personality features. I stopped doing that the moment I began to understand a little about my handicap. It was a great relief not to have to imitate—I no longer feel I am a poor copy of a person. I no longer feel I have to be so fraudulent in order to prevent other people from noticing that I'm not quite ordinary. And I no longer have so many vague problems I feel I have to hide. This has released energy, and I feel I can cope with much more than before.

I still have a bent—I like that word—for curved things, but it's no longer a fixation. It comes out mostly in things like finding I want to make a detour in order to take a road that bends instead of a straight one, or feeling a desire to touch something that is beautifully curved. It is good that I can choose to allow myself a detour, to enjoy that curve, but that I can also choose not to if I think I haven't the time. And I know when it's all right to touch whatever arouses my desire to touch and when not, and I don't find it difficult not to. I think it somehow feels as if my attachment to curves comes from being so 'straight' inside. It's because my nervous system is rectilinear that I need to acquire a curve from outside. As if, when I really need an inner curve so as not to be so rigid, I have to find it somewhere outside myself.

How, then, did I become so 'fantastically well' or so unhandicapped? How did it come about that several of my difficulties have become so much less prominent, that I do not give an impression of autism? I don't know. I don't feel fantastically well. I am quite ambivalent when it comes to my handicap. I'm happy with what I've got and sad about what I lack. Though sometimes an ability I'm happy to have and which not for the life of me would I want to be without—my sharp vision, for instance—can also have a dark side that saddens me. I'm capable of feeling 'I don't want to be like you' and of thinking I have the right to be different, that I like being otherwise. And at the same time, I still want to be a real person through and through and can wish that I could be transformed or that I had been born someone else.

I think my ability to retreat into myself has in many

situations proved a good safeguard. This does not mean that I have developed it as a strategy to protect myself, as a certain therapist would say. I simply had the bad luck to be born with a biological handicap and, in addition, into a dysfunctional family. I would be considerably more neurotic, I think, if I hadn't had this handicap. It is also possible that the fact that I have had to manage on my own has made me less handicapped, and it may have been of some benefit to me that I have had to communicate with other people. So perhaps I would have been more autistic in a more normal family, but then maybe, also, I would have been happier. No one can know.

My family are exceptional in many ways, but I think children in more ordinary families are also affected by events similar to those I had to face. Despite everything, my parents weren't monsters. They were considered by society to be fairly ordinary, though it has to be said that society didn't often happen to look in on them when they were knocking each other about. But nonetheless, although my mother was more damaged than most mothers and my father was colder and more egoistic than most fathers, I think many of their mistakes were rather ordinary.

My need to bite and my desire to bite into people have gone. All that vanished at some point when I was twenty-four or twenty-five, and I miss it slightly. It was actually a pleasure and also a funny side of my personality—being the kind of person who asked permission to bite people. Not just anyone, of course. I confined myself to those who might be expected to answer yes.

I thought that steady shudder down my spine had also gone, but during this last year it has come back. It went away for many years—it must be ten years since I last felt it. To cheer myself up, I tell myself that perhaps certain symptoms to do with this handicap will appear again as I develop and get better. Though I don't really know for sure. Anyway, I can now deal with the spine shudder. I am grown up and I can reason with myself about what I feel and what I shall do about it. Sometimes a hot shower can help. At other times, it's a matter of just putting up with the feeling until it goes away. On the other hand, the sensitivity at the nape of my neck has remained to this day. Although I've tolerated being touched more and more over the years, the back of my neck has remained forbidden territory. It has been so incredibly sensitive, but in recent years it has also become more and more normal, almost like any other part of my body. I can even tolerate having a shoulder and neck massage, previously an absolute impossibility.

Although I still find it difficult to work out other people's intentions, I think I am more aware of whether I like someone, and in what way. Previously I thought it was a question of opposites, that I liked someone only if that person aroused my antipathy. I have grown up with my inner reality being so totally different from my external reality, and I have thought that was as it should be. I also thought that other people knew better than what my feelings were telling me, and so I sought out those who wanted to tell me something different. I don't do that any longer. Whenever I used to seek out people I deep down didn't like, I would use up a great deal of energy looking for their good sides, thereby achieving that divided sense of both loathing and liking, and ending up in a destructive relationship with them. I cannot say I was conscious of all this, but at the back of my mind I was aware of it. I thought it seemed sick, this whole business of liking and disliking. But there was so much else in the world that seemed sick—I had simply learnt that that was how it should be. Furthermore, I didn't know whether this was wrong, or how things might be different.

I have also had a tendency to try to 'convert' people

who don't like me. It's never been important to me whether people liked me, so this was not some urge to be loved by everyone. But I thought in a somewhat inverted way that it was only with my 'enemies' that I ought to be friends. I don't know whether perhaps the feeling of emotional incompatibility had to be part of it all. I never went to any great lengths to get them to like me. I was never desperate. I just accepted their view of me, then turned it 180 degrees, calmly and quietly. And I felt some satisfaction when I succeeded. I probably, unfortunately, also thought I was doing them a service, modifying their narrow-mindedness. Nowadays I no longer have even an ounce of energy over for people I know don't like me.

I am still somewhat uncertain about how things hang together. Although nowadays I can explain things intellectually to myself, I am not always emotionally convinced. I'm still not quite certain that the parents who fetched me that day from my grandparents' really were the same ones I had had before. I am not convinced—although naturally I know in my mind that they *were* the same parents I'd had all the time, that people don't exist in several similar versions.

Certain metal objects still make my stomach turn over, and I still dislike touching jewellery. But I can stand some smooth and simple jewellery made of leather and stones. On the other hand, I have no aversion to people wearing jewellery, as a psychologist wrote in a report about me. People can wear what they like, but if they take their jewellery off and put it down on a table, I find that slightly unpleasant. Then I'm intensely aware of it lying there all the time. Generally speaking, most things to do with jewellery are bearable as long as I don't have to touch it—except, possibly, for going into a knick-knack shop full of metal jewellery, which can at once cause me nausea. I have to wait outside if I am with someone who wants to go into that kind of shop.

When I was in therapy, a great many hours were spent interpreting my distaste for jewellery. Of course, I wondered why I had it, and I very much wanted to understand it, although it was not a directly disabling phobia. It was something to do with my earliest wanting to be a woman, the therapist believed. She asked me what I thought about it.

'Maybe. I don't know,' I said.

'All little girls want to dress up in their mothers' clothes and jewellery,' she went on, and explained that something must have happened that had made me decide that I didn't want to be the same kind of person as my mother, that I didn't want to be a woman after all.

This sounded logical. I had no sense of wanting to be like my mother. But I couldn't recall that as a child I had felt that I *didn't* want to be like her, either. To me it seemed that I had never given the matter a thought. But according to the therapist, this was due to my suppression of those emotions, because it had been so difficult for me to feel them. Well, what did I know? The arguments were perfectly possible and intellectually satisfying, except that they said nothing to me emotionally. They really said nothing whatsoever to me.

'Oh, well, maybe,' I said, and then we would begin all over again from the beginning.

The therapist often talked about what all little girls thought and felt, but I was never able to recognise myself in what she said. And yet, I had more faith in her than in what I felt. She was the expert, after all, and I had probably forgotten all those feelings she said all little girls had.

Now I know that it's just that I have a strong feeling of unpleasantness in jewellery, and that it is probably sheer chance that it's about jewellery in particular, and certain buttons, that I feel like this. There are others with the same kind of handicap as mine who have an inexplicable fear of something or other. And nor is it entirely unusual to experience strange signals from within your body—nausea, in my case—triggered by things other people don't react to at all.

One problem with psychodynamic approaches to people appears to centre on something my therapist used to say—'It's possible to understand everything.' I actually don't know whether I should think she was right or wrong about that. Perhaps it's possible to understand everything, but then I believe it requires more knowledge than any one person can possess, regardless of how knowledgeable he or she may be.

To be normally polite still requires a constant effort on my part. I never seem to be able to get those standard phrases to come out by themselves. I don't know what it is that other people do that enables them to answer automatically 'Thanks, the same to you' when someone wishes them a nice weekend. I have to think all the time and remember what I'm expected to say. Sometimes when I'm rather tired, I forget and give whoever has asked me a long and detailed answer to the question 'How are you?' Then I forget to ask back how he or she is, because when I don't think all the time about how I am supposed to behave, it's quite logical for me never to ask about something I am not interested in knowing.

It is also hard work distinguishing the questions 'How *are* you?' and 'How are *you?*', and deciding how much of an answer I am to give. I think I often answer more honestly than the questioner has intended. I can be nonplussed sometimes when I've asked how someone is and then am asked the same in return. As the person I've asked presumably feels that I'm really interested in knowing how he or she is, I often get a detailed answer back and that feels good. But I can't help thinking it seems rather impolite if they then just routinely return the question without being truly interested in my state of health.

Once I have heard how the other person really is, I don't feel any special desire to start talking about myself. I wonder if other people do? I don't think so, and yet one is expected to behave like this. Deep down inside me, I sometimes get so tired—you have such complicated rules in your world! And all the time I have to think and think and think about them.